Thursdays with Zoe

UNFORGETTABLE STORIES OF ALZHEIMER'S,
FAMILY, AND FAITH

April Perry

Published by April and Eric Perry from *LearnDoBecome.com*
Front Cover Photography by Rachel Tucker at *RachelClare.com*
Back Cover Photography by Melanie Wilson
Printed in the United States of America
First Edition 2016

Thursdays with Zoe / April Perry. —1st ed.
ISBN 978-1537501277

Contents

To my mother, Zoe:

*Although you can no longer remember
the stories in this book, I am keeping them safe
for you and sharing your light with the world.*

Acknowledgments

The opportunity to write this book has been a gift—from several beautiful people in my life.

First, to my husband, Eric, for believing in this project from the very beginning. He bought me a big poster board and stacks of sticky notes so I could brainstorm the various chapters, he sent me off to a hotel once a month and cared for our home and family so I could have quiet time to write, and he held me tight every time I returned from one of my visits to my parents' home...knowing how much I needed his strength. Eric, I love you with all my heart.

Next, to my four precious children, Alia, Grace, Ethan, and Spencer. You have lived many of these stories with me, and you fill my life with a joy I can't describe. Thank you for loving me in spite of my imperfections, thank you for being by my side while we are losing Grandma, and thank you for showing me the power of a family on a daily basis. You give me *such* great hope for the future.

An enormous thanks to my parents, Robert and Zoe Wilson. My mother obviously inspired the main content of this book, but my father has been our steady support through all of this. He listened to each of my stories about Mom and shared his own memoirs and photos with us during each visit. He now sits by my mom's bed each day and shows us what it means to truly devote your life to another person. I adore him.

And to my brothers and sisters, in-laws, nieces, nephews, and extended family who have come together during this time and offered tremendous support. I love hearing about your experiences with Mom and seeing how you continue her legacy. Thank you for reading the drafts of my chapters and letting me come to you when I need a listening ear.

To my mother-in-law, Peggy Perry, who has cared for me and my family when my own mother could not. It means so much to know you are there.

I am also so grateful to Saren Eyre Loosli, my partner at Power of Moms who has totally supported my dream of writing books, and our entire Power of Moms team who inspire me every day to strengthen families.

The specifics of this book would not have been possible without the help of a whole team. Much gratitude to Rachel Nielsen, who read through my entire manuscript with the love and care of a friend who also has gone through the process of losing an angel mother. Thank you to Rachel Tucker for voluntarily offering to photograph my mother and I together. I couldn't think of a better cover for this book! And another huge thanks to my sister-in-law Melanie Wilson for the photo on the back cover, which features *most* of our still-growing family and captured a happy moment when Mom still knew our names.

The design services from Design Pickle have been an incredible blessing as we've prepared the book cover, eBook files, and digital images for the website and social media sharing. And Catherine Baduin, who formatted the manuscript for publication, treated each chapter with more care than I ever expected. It thrilled me to see everything come together.

LearnDoBecome.com would not be the same without our fantastic assistant, Danielle Porter, who takes care of the many details of the website—including the preparation of all of our book files and pages—while tenderly caring for our thousands of community members. Danielle, we appreciate you more than we can say!

Finally, I offer my gratitude to all my friends online who have followed this story for years and left comments via my websites and social networks. Thank you for caring about our family, for lending me your strength, and for doing so much good where you are. I am blessed beyond measure.

Introduction

I have done my very best in the pages of this book to capture the most beautiful light I know in order to help you along your way.

My mother, Zoe, is in the final stages of Alzheimer's Disease, but this isn't a book "about" Alzheimer's. Rather, this is a book about you. It's a book about *each* of us, and who we are becoming in the context of our family lives. Whether or not you have a loved one with Alzheimer's, if you care about what you are learning, what you are doing, and who you are becoming, this book will hopefully lift your spirit and improve your perspective.

My mom's Alzheimer's started a few years ago when she began to forget minor details—like where she had put her phone or who had come to visit her that day. Then she started forgetting *major* things, like how to drive herself home or which bank held all the money she and my dad had saved. I still remember the first day she couldn't recall the names of all her children—because my name was one that she'd forgotten. And now, as I write, she is in bed full time because her legs have forgotten how to stand.

With millions of people suffering from Alzheimer's, our situation isn't entirely unique, but I have felt a consistent call to write this book, and I'd like to explain the "why" a little bit more.

A few years ago, I wrote an article for my Power of Moms website called "Your Children Want YOU!" That article, which talks about how we too often compare ourselves to what we see on social media and forget that the *real* power in our families comes from who we are, was read by more than two million people and included the first public mention of my mom's memory loss (we didn't know then that it was Alzheimer's).

Since that time, as I have continued to write about our family's experiences and the powerful lessons my mother taught me, I've discovered that the story of her life isn't something I can keep to myself. People who have similar feelings of adoration for their mothers seem to want someone to put words to what they feel. And people who have painful memories of their mothers want to know how they can break the cycle in their own families. (These are brave, beautiful souls.)

Their comments and emails got me thinking:

> *What, exactly, did my mother do that inspired her eight children—every single one of us—to love her with all our hearts? And how can that be replicated?*

I don't think anyone can pinpoint an exact moment or a single idea that explains how a relationship "happens." Loving another person can theoretically be *explained* all day long, but it looks different for everyone. What *is* the same, however, is how it *feels*. And while each family's experiences will be unique, the incredible power that comes when love is at the center of our lives can so *easily* be replicated.

This book illustrates what my mother's love felt like to me, and it explains how I am trying my absolute best to keep that beauty and goodness going in my own family.

I started this book timidly—with just a few notes here and there. Then as my mom's health slowly started to decline, I decided to write a new section by each Thursday so I could read it to her during my weekly visits.

As her decline became more rapid, however, I stopped writing. I felt like I didn't have time and that maybe I should wait until she returned to God. And *then* I could write.

But on one particular visit to my mother's bedside, the instructions came clearly:

> *April, you need to make this record. There is time for you to write. It will be a gift for you to read it to her. And even though she may appear not to know what you are reading, she will know. And she will feel the love you have for her. And she will see clearly that her work in this life has been worth it.*

So I started writing more diligently--imperfectly at best--because I don't think it is possible to adequately capture the *immense* love I feel for my mother and for her lasting influence on my life. And there *has* been time. More than I ever expected. I feel like the heavens paused for just a moment so that this book could happen.

As I am putting the finishing touches on this manuscript, she is doing beautifully. She smiles when I see her, and she hugs and kisses me on each visit—even though she's not quite sure who I am. The other day, on one of my visits, I said, "My name is April. I'm your daughter!" She looked at me like I had just given her an amazing gift and exclaimed with absolute wonder, "You ARE?"

It was sweet. A little sad, but mostly sweet.

At this point you may be wondering if this book is for *you*.

Maybe.

I hope so.

But in all honesty, this is what I am doing:

1. I'm writing for my Creator. This book is about becoming someone who God trusts. And while the stories and principles are applicable to people of all religions (or no religion) my

number one goal is to write something that is acceptable to the One I believe created me.

2. I'm writing for my mom, who smiles and laughs when she hears the stories, adamantly insists that she does *not* have Alzheimer's, and then can't remember any of our conversations even 30 seconds later. That's okay. I have a feeling that someday she will be given the gift of remembering all the Thursdays we spent together, and we can go through this book from beginning to end!

3. I'm writing for me. I'm not going to pretend like I've been strong through this whole process. Pouring my heart into a book is really therapeutic for me. I *need* to write. It helps me to capture her voice and her wisdom that I can't bear the thought of losing. My sweet husband made huge sacrifices every month for more than two years to give me the chance to record this. He knew the time to process all of these thoughts would help me. I can't thank him enough.

4. I'm writing for our children (and grandchildren). This thought keeps coming back over and over again. I want to record these precious memories for Alia, Grace, Ethan, Spencer, and the future souls that will come after them so when *they* need strength and encouragement—at every stage of their lives—it will be waiting for them.

5. I'm writing for "that person" who needs this.

Every once in awhile I get a message from someone who lives far away--who I never would have met in a million years had it not been for the things that I write and publish. The message usually says something like this: "Thank you for writing. Please don't stop. It makes a difference for me." (If *you're* that person, I send you my love.)

You'll notice that there's a question and a challenge at the end of each chapter. These are simply my suggestions to help you put these ideas into practice (and you will most likely come up with your own ideas that are even better!). We all know that reading a book does very little for us unless we actually apply what we learn. Please consider these suggestions as cues to take a step back, consider what you have felt, and identify one way you can make your life just a little better because of what you read.

Now just one more thing before I get going: While I will be sharing my favorite stories about my mom, please don't get confused and think she was perfect. She would feel sad about that. She was a "real" person— with struggles and weaknesses just like the rest of us, and never in a million years would she ask for all of this attention. In fact, she would completely shy away from it and say, "Oh, people don't want to read about *me!*" That isn't true, however. It's just that I don't think she has ever been able to see how remarkable she truly is.

My life has been deeply impacted by this incredible woman—and now it's your turn.

Thank you for reading this book and allowing me to open my heart in such a tender way. It is an honor to share my mother with you.

With love,

April

Your Children Want YOU!

There's this crazy phenomenon going on right now. Good, devoted mothers get on Pinterest (and blogs, and Facebook, and other social media), and then they flip through parenting magazines and TV channels (full of advertisements and media hype), and they're convinced they're not enough.

They're convinced that everyone else has magnetic, alphabetized spice containers, and unless their garden parties are thematically accessorized with butterfly lanterns, *and* they're wearing the latest fashions (in a size two, of course), there's no point in even showing up for the day.

Last Saturday, this happened to me. I came home from a lovely day out with my extended family and had serious intentions to spend the evening making a craft for an upcoming holiday and trying out a new recipe. By the time I got everyone settled and fed, however, I was so tired that I just laid on the couch and dozed while my children played and got themselves to bed.

Around 8:30, when I finally had the energy to sit up, I decided to try out Pinterest for a few minutes until my husband got home. There it was- a thousand reasons why I'm failing at all things domestic. I don't make grilled cheese sandwiches look like ice cream. I don't even have seasonal throw pillows on my couches or live plants *anywhere* in the house. Is it really so hard? Can't I pull myself together and wrap some candles in green foliage and bring happiness to our decor with bright fabrics and hand-crafted photo frames?

As I was trying to calm my frenzied state of mind, my husband came home and held me tight. We talked about our day, and he told me how much he loves me and that he wants our boys to marry someone like me. I fell asleep snuggled under his arm.

The following morning, our children enthusiastically bounded into our bedroom and tucked themselves into our covers. My four-year-old gave me an arm massage, and we all sat there together—joking, laughing, planning the day ahead, and enjoying that special feeling of family.

Reflecting on the discouragement I'd felt the night before, I realized that my family doesn't care about what I see on Pinterest. They care about *me*.

My daughter Grace loves me to sing "Baby Mine" to her each night before bed. When I go out of town, she misses that special ritual. We have recordings of Michael Crawford and Allison Krauss singing their versions, but Grace doesn't want those. She wants me. So I recorded myself singing "Baby Mine" and emailed the audio file to her and to my husband so Grace can hear "her song" before she sleeps. As far as she's concerned, my untrained voice belongs at the top of the charts.

A few months ago, I was practicing sideways Dutch braids on my two daughters. They had found these great "how-to" videos online, and we set up our comb, brush, and hair bands in front of the computer so I could become an expert. Half-way through the braid, my fingers got all tangled up, the hair was too loose, and one of my daughters had been sitting with her head to the side for several minutes.

Feeling extremely frustrated, I said, "That little girl in the video is so lucky to have a mom who knows how to do hair." My daughter stopped me in my tracks when she responded, "But I have a mom who is trying."

My mom is in her 70s, and her memory is starting to go. Her sweetness and love are as strong as ever, but when we talk on the phone, she can't remember the last time we spoke or the last time we saw each other. At the end of one phone call a few weeks ago, I whispered, "I miss you, Mom."

She said, "Oh, I miss you, too! But we'll get together soon. You can come down to the park, and we'll get an ice cream cone at McDonald's."

I replied, "Yes, that will be fun." But then the tears started, and I had to use every ounce of control to keep my voice even so she wouldn't know I was crying.

What I *really* meant was, "I miss being able to talk to you, Mom. I miss laying on the grass while my children make a hopscotch and savoring our long phone conversations. I miss you remembering all those secrets I used to tell you. I miss you asking me if I'm okay. I miss seeing you read books and hearing you sing while you do the dishes and having you drive out to my house without getting lost. I miss you remembering how much I need you."

My mother didn't specialize in home decor or gourmet cooking, and she didn't lift weights or run marathons. But she makes me feel like I am the most important, wonderful person ever born. If I could pick any mother in the whole world, it would be *my* mom.

There's something deeper going on in family life than can ever be expressed on a social network. Whatever it is we feel we are lacking, can we collectively decide–as deliberate mothers–that we are not going to sit around feeling discouraged about all the things we're not? Can we remind each other that it is our uniqueness and love that our children long for?

It is our voices. Our smiles. Our jiggly tummies. Of course we want to learn, improve, exercise, cook better, make our homes lovelier, and provide beautiful experiences for our children, but at the end of the day, our children don't want a discouraged, stressed-out mom who is wishing she were someone else.

If *you* ever find yourself looking in the mirror at a woman who feels badly that she hasn't yet made flower-shaped soap, please offer her this helpful reminder: "Your children want *you!*"

> ➤ **QUESTION:** How can you best remember how important you are to your family in the midst of so many temptations to compare yourself with others?

> ➤ **CHALLENGE:** Recognize any tendencies you might have to get wrapped up in discouragement, and set up a regular way to remind yourself that your children want *you.*

Lessons on Love

CHAPTER 1

The Street Sweeper is Coming!!

Whose keeper are we?

In the little seaside community where I was raised, the street sweeper was a *big* deal. It barreled down one side of the street at noon every Thursday, the other side at noon every Friday.

Because the houses were so close together, very few families had driveways (ours was awkwardly positioned and could only hold one car), and because our garage was absolutely full of stuff, parking the car in there had never been an option. (I didn't know people actually parked their cars in garages until I was in college.)

This situation left us consistently scrambling to move our cars...or get a $50 ticket from the merciless ticket truck that followed minutes behind in the street sweeper's tracks.

Well, something about this whole process put my mom into a panic. At two minutes 'til noon every Thursday and Friday, the street sweeper would sit at the top of the street and wait, and when the clock struck the hour, everyone within 200 yards could hear the motor begin to roar.

My mother's heart would jump wildly in her chest. She would stop whatever she was doing, and she would run outside just to make *sure* we had moved our cars (which we typically had...). However, once she got outside, she would also take a peek up and down the street to make sure everyone *else* had moved their cars, and if they hadn't, she would run as

13

APRIL PERRY

fast as she could (never very fast) to their front doors, knock and ring as though there were a fire, and urgently warn them, "The street sweeper is coming!!"

That's how we got to know the names of practically all of our neighbors, and they all knew Zoe—the woman who collectively saved them hundreds and thousands of dollars a year on street sweeping tickets. (One time my mom whispered to me, "I bet the city doesn't like me very much because I prevent them from giving out so many tickets, but that's not right for them to charge such high prices if someone forgets to move a car. It's not right at all.)

Now this lesson in itself was powerful to me—the idea that neighbors watch out for each other and warn each other when "danger" is approaching, but I will *never* forget the day my mom took it to a whole new level.

A man across the street had *just* moved in to our neighborhood, and one day his car was sitting on the wrong side of the street, exactly when the street sweeper was revving its engine.

No amount of knocking or ringing worked…he simply wasn't home.

My mom waited out by his car, and as soon as the street sweeper reached her, she approached the driver and said sweetly, "Please, this man just moved here, and I really don't want him to get a ticket. That's not a very nice way to welcome him to the neighborhood."

The man driving the roaring machine was brusque and not in the mood to be bothered. He replied, "Well, I'm sorry, but I can't clean the street where his car is parked."

Seeing that she wasn't going to get anywhere from this angle, she said, "Will you at least not call this in to your ticket person?"

He widened his eyes, shocked that she knew how the system worked (my mom was sneaky!), and then he gave her a little sideways smile before proceeding on his way.

At that point, my mom sprang into action. She bolted across the street, grabbed the hose from the side of our house, turned on the water—full power—and stretched it as far as it could go across the street.

She sprayed that street, under and around our neighbor's car, so that there was no way you could tell if the street sweeper had been there or not.

Then she quickly returned the hose to its place, ran back into the house, hid behind the curtains of our front window (peeking out *just* enough to see what the ticket man would do), and waited.

Within a couple of minutes, the ticket truck pulled up behind the parked car...and sat there for quite awhile.

Had the street sweeper already cleaned that section? Did the car get parked there in the two minutes before he had arrived on that street?

(I'm *sure* my mom was praying as she watched this whole process from behind the curtains.)

The ticket man got out of his car, walked around the offending vehicle, bent down to look underneath, surveyed the wetness on the whole street to try to identify any out-of-place street sweeping tracks, and then stood there and scratched his head...totally puzzled.

Not one hundred percent sure if the car deserved a ticket or not, and apparently not having received a call from the street sweeper himself (yay!), the ticket man got back into his truck and drove away.

For my mom, this was VICTORY!

I think of this story often, and I'm continually trying to find ways to carry on this tradition. My kids and I even posted street sweeper "warning signs" at the entrances to our neighborhood for awhile, but I've come to understand that this was about more than avoiding tickets. It was about truly caring for neighbors and understanding that life isn't just about looking out for "number one."

I don't know how it is for you, but I personally have a tricky time getting past the needs within the walls of my own home. Cleaning the house, answering emails, running to appointments, shopping, completing my work responsibilities...I can go for days or weeks without talking to a neighbor at all.

But there's something about life that feels safer, calmer, more exciting, less lonely, and more like a team effort when you consciously put the interests of your neighbors as a priority in your life. It's a powerful feeling when you realize that you're not alone in the world—that you're part of a community that looks out for each other. But that kind of a community— that kind of a family—doesn't just happen. It's deliberately created through kind acts of service given without any hope of reward. This street sweeper story is just one of many that illustrate my moms's tender (and sometimes humorous) care for those around her. In everything she did, my mother taught me that we are each other's keepers.

> ➤ **QUESTION:** What could you do to create a stronger sense of community and neighborly love? What has worked in the past? How can you do more of that?

> ➤ **CHALLENGE:** Think for a moment about your current neighborhood and identify a simple way you could help someone or get to know another neighbor better.

CHAPTER 2

Oh! That's My LAY-deeeee!

Who deserves our love and respect?

When I was in high school, our booster club had a special fundraiser where they sold "Bruin Cards" that enabled families to receive discounts at several local fast food restaurants.

My mother thought this was *genius*. She especially liked taking us to El Pollo Loco for their "buy one, get one free" burritos after we'd had a busy day at school.

One evening at five, after my drama rehearsal had finished, my mom took me over to the El Pollo Loco drive-thru. When it was her turn to order, she leaned out the window toward the microphone on the order box and said in her cute way—kind of slow and kind of loud, so as not to be misunderstood—"Hello! I would like a Classic Chicken Burrito, buy one get one free with the Bruin Card."

The woman who responded through the speaker sounded *elated*—beyond anything I had ever heard (or have *yet* to hear) in a drive-thru lane.

"Oh!" she cried out, like she was greeting a long-lost friend. "That's my LAY-deeeee!"

I sat in the passenger seat, speechless.

> *What has my mom been doing over here that would elicit that kind of response? How did she get to the point that the cashier at El Pollo Loco wouldn't only recognize her voice, but would be utterly excited to see her?*

As our car crept through the line, I peppered my mom with questions. Her response was so casual. "This is my friend who is just so nice...."

I finally met the lady when we picked up our burritos. My mom introduced us. The woman was in her mid-twenties, physically as opposite in appearance from my mom as one can get. But their twin smiles and beautiful souls had somehow connected. "Your mom is so sweet," she told me.

This experience at the drive-thru has stayed with me, but it wasn't until just a couple of years ago that I saw one of these unique interactions in person.

Although my mom's Alzheimer's was starting to progress at that point, she still liked to answer the phone, and no one could stop her.

One afternoon while I was visiting, I heard this after the phone rang:

"Hello!" she greeted the caller happily.

Then after listening for a few moments, she replied, "Well, I'm not sure, but let me check."

"Bob!" she called into the next room, "Do we need a new roof?"

My dad, trying to be patient, but getting a little agitated with my mother's constant questions, replied, "No, Zoe. We do *not* need a new roof. We just had ours fixed a few years ago."

I listened *very* carefully at that point—wondering how my mother would explain her answer to the salesman.

"I'm sorry," she began with a truly apologetic tone. "But my husband is a *party pooper.*"

I tried my best not to laugh.

"But you have *such* a nice voice," she continued, "and I wish you the very best with your sales."

With that, they ended the call, and I sat still...stunned.

While I would have briskly replied, "I'm sorry, we don't accept sales calls. Please take our number off your list," my mother continually showed us through her actions that *every* person we meet deserves our love and respect.

These two experiences weren't the anomalies. They simply represent the entire framework from which my mother operated.

As a result, even though she got pulled over by police officers eight times throughout her life, she never once got a ticket.

Store clerks and postal carriers would go out of their way to make sure she was well taken care of, and practically every time she got on the phone to address an issue with an insurance or utility company, she got what she needed—simply because she was *so nice to them.*

I've spent years trying to replicate my mother's art. I want to be just like her.

But each time I asked her to clarify her process, she seemed confused by my question. "Oh, April," she would say, "Everybody wants to do a kindness! Each person in the world has good in them, and they're just looking for a reason to share that goodness. All I do is give them the opportunity to do so! I explain what I need, I treat them with love, and I show them how their kindness will help me. They are excited for the chance to make that kind choice."

As one of the main purposes of this book is to identify what, exactly, my mother did that bonded each of us so tightly to her, I can't emphasize this point enough:

When you treat others with love, respect, and kindness—no matter *who* they are and regardless of whether or not they can do anything for you—your children will be watching closely. They will want to be like

19

you, they will feel safe and protected around you, and if a time ever comes when you need them to care for you, they will feel *honored* to do so because it is their *privilege* to do a kindness.

> ➤ **QUESTION:** Is there an area in your life where you could be more kind? (Particularly with someone who isn't in a position to help you "get ahead"?)

> ➤ **CHALLENGE:** The next time you have the choice to treat another person with kindness or contempt, choose kindness (and watch what happens!).

CHAPTER 3

The Casserole that Changed My Heart

If you can't fix it, what do you do?

My little brother used to play with a couple of boys who lived a few streets over from us. They mostly played video games together and ate scrambled eggs and toast from the trays my mom would prepare for them after school.

We didn't know their family very well (or really, at all), but the boys were quiet and respectful, and they liked being at our house.

One afternoon, my mom was driving home from her errands, and she had a little bit of extra time. She considered dropping by my sister's house to do an exercise video with her or running by another store, but then she stopped and offered a brief prayer: *How can I be an instrument today?*

The idea came into her mind to drop by the home of the family I mentioned above. It was kind of an uncomfortable thing to do, but my mom knocked at the door, and when the boys' mother answered, my mom asked her how she was doing.

"Not very well," she replied.

In the conversation that followed, she confided to my mom that things were *dreadfully* wrong with her marriage. Things were stressful with their family dynamics, and her husband had threatened to leave her.

Through her tears, she explained that she didn't know what to do, and her whole life was a mess.

I've theoretically put myself into my mom's situation a few times. *What would I do if a neighbor opened up to me about that kind of a problem?*

Most of us don't want to get involved in something so hard and so personal. We're all busy with our own lives, and challenges like that are obviously built up over the course of many years. Replying with, "Oh, I'm so sorry. I hope things work out okay," doesn't cut it. But you can't just insert yourself into other people's lives and try to fix things for them.

Well, my mother handled it beautifully:

She put her arm around our neighbor's shoulder and said enthusiastically, "Now here's what we're going to do. You're going to work really hard this afternoon and get your house all clean and shiny. And I'm going to go back to my house and make you a nice dinner that you can serve to your husband when he gets home."

"Oh, I can't possibly let you do that," she responded.

"He doesn't even need to know the meal was from me. Now what time does he get home?" my mom replied insistently.

"About 5:30."

"Okay, I'll be here at 5. And once he gets home and sees how beautiful the house looks and gets to eat a nice hot meal, then you're going to have the boys go play outside, and you're going to sit down together and have a good talk about how you can make things work and how you can take care of your family."

For the rest of the afternoon, my mom and I (an 11-year-old girl, at the time) prepared a special casserole and baked some homemade bread. As we worked, my mom relayed the story to me.

Then we put all the warm food into a cardboard box, nestled onto my favorite tablecloth--the one with the cherries on it.

I remember looking at the red and blue designs of the cloth and protesting, "But what if we don't get it back?"

"We don't worry about those kinds of things, April," she responded. (But, yes, we did get it back.)

Checking the box once more to make sure everything was ready, my mom carried it out to the car and placed it on my lap in the passenger seat while she drove the half mile to their home. The warmth from the casserole settled into me as we travelled, but I remember feeling worried—worried that this casserole wasn't enough to save a whole marriage. I remember giving a sideways glance to my mother, but she was so happy and so confident that God would help take care of that family that I didn't say anything.

Once we got to the house, I waited in the car, and my mom took the box up to the door. It was a quick drop, and to be perfectly honest, I'm not sure what ever happened to that family.

I know...you were probably hoping to hear a miraculous ending, but that really isn't the point of this story.

The point, to me, is about what happened in the hearts of at least two of the people involved.

It must have done *something* for that struggling mother to know that someone cared about her. We all know how a simple act of kindness can restore your faith in the world--and your faith in yourself.

And I can tell you with 100% certainty what it did to the 11-year-old girl sitting in the car--because I clearly remember that experience more than 25 years later.

For one thing, I remember thinking that I wanted to be just like my mom.

She never told a soul about that dinner, and she didn't do it for praise. She did it out of pure love. Watching her mix the bread dough and working side by side with her as we assembled that casserole, I could see she was happy when she was serving. It was ingrained in her, and I decided at that moment that I wanted to make that a part of *my* identity, as well.

She also taught me that it's okay if we can't solve everyone's problems. It feels like too much sometimes...seeing families disintegrating around us, hearing stories of neglect and abuse. But you and I have a responsibility to remember that while we clearly can't fix every challenge out there, we can do *something*.

> ➤ *QUESTION:* Is there a situation of which you're aware right now that feels overwhelming to fix?

> ➤ *CHALLENGE:* Sit down and identify just one thing you *could* do to show that person/those people that you care about them.

CHAPTER 4

Nail-Painting Parties Under a Tree

When is there time for service?

During the summers when I was six and seven, a local elementary school had a half-day program when we could play games in the cafeteria, make lanyards and other crafts, join a softball team, and enjoy time with our friends.

My mom would drop us off for several hours at a time, and we loved it. Sometimes she would come in for a few minutes, and sometimes she would bring a blanket and read under a tree while we played a little while longer. Those were precious memories.

There was a little girl at the school who played with us sometimes (I'll call her Audrey), and while I didn't notice anything different about her, my mom sensed that something wasn't quite right.

One afternoon, I saw my mom speaking with her—gently asking a few questions.

I walked up to them to see what was going on. "Why is my mom talking to Audrey?" I remember thinking...a little embarrassed.

When I got close enough to hear their conversation, they were just finishing up. Audrey was looking down at her hands, examining her well-bitten fingernails, and my mom was giving her some kind of reminder: "Remember, I'll be here next week!"

With that, Audrey ran off to play, and I looked up at my mom—totally perplexed.

Mom put her arm around me and started walking me out to the car. "I've noticed that Audrey needs a little bit of extra love, so today I told her that she has *beautiful* nail beds, and if she can go for one week without biting her nails, I will bring my nail polish here to the school and give her a manicure."

My thoughts were anything but kind at that point. "What about *my* nail beds? Weren't they beautiful? When was the last time you painted *my* nails, Mom?"

But then I stopped—first realizing that I didn't actually *like* nail polish and that I always picked it off when my mom applied it for me. And *second*, I started to sense that there was something going on that I couldn't fully understand.

A week passed, and Audrey didn't bite her nails once.

She came running up to my mom on the morning of the promised manicure—waving her fingers proudly to show off the tiny crescents that had grown over the tops of her fingers throughout the course of the week.

My mom smiled, brought out a plastic box filled with her nail polish selection, and spread out her blanket under a tree about 20 yards from the school cafeteria, where I was playing with my sister.

I remember looking out the window, watching my mom paint Audrey's nails. I saw the smiles, and I still remember feeling a twinge of jealousy. But as I observed that loving act of service and contemplated what it must have meant to that little girl, I remember thinking, "Audrey gets to have my mom for a few minutes. I get to have her forever."

Now sometimes when I reflect on these moments—these powerful examples of love and service that my mom set for me—I feel like I am falling short.

When do *I* do things like this? How many little girls have I passed by who would have *loved* to have their nails painted by me? Am I just selfish to never have noticed? Is that so sad that I don't even own *one* bottle of nail polish?

Please, if you're feeling any of that, let's just agree to *both* stop it. Because this is what I think my mom would want us to remember:

Serving others doesn't have to be something we plan. It is often something we do "along the way." It's not about trying to replicate others' gifts (because I still don't like painting nails...). It's about being *aware*, looking for those who could use a little more love, and then figuring out a simple way to *offer* that love.

I think of Audrey often—her smile when she looked down at her beautiful nails, the careful way she played for the rest of the day so she wouldn't ruin the shine of the polish, and most of all, how cherished she felt when she was being cared for by a loving mother.

I hope that things in her own family improved, as I totally lost track of her after that. But regardless of Audrey's circumstances, we get to choose every single day to *make* the time to serve.

> ➤ **QUESTION:** Do you feel pressed for time whenever you think about giving service? What experiences have you had "serving along the way"?

> ➤ **CHALLENGE:** Keep your eyes open for service opportunities that open up right around you...and find at least one way this week to give a little part of yourself to a person in need.

CHAPTER 5

Wigs, Stakeouts, and Sleeping in a Doorway

How much of ourselves should we be willing to give?

Our neighbor Carol had the best dress-up clothes.

Mom always sent us down to her house before Halloween, and Carol would let us dig through her costume trunk—trying on fake furs, velvet hats, and high-heeled shoes. I still get a little giddy just thinking about it.

One day, Mom took me over to Carol's house to look through the costumes, but this time it wasn't for *me*. My mom needed a wig.

I remember looking at my mom quizzically as she tried on wig after wig while observing her reflection in Carol's bathroom mirror.

"Mom, what are you *doing*?" I asked.

"Shhhh," she whispered gently. "I'll talk with you about it later."

Well, "later" finally came, and while this is a story I need to share delicately, I feel like it's one that must be recorded.

You see, my mom had a dear friend who was concerned that her husband was having an affair. He wasn't coming home at night—claiming to be sleeping at one of their other properties—and she didn't know what to do. She had turned to my mom, her trusted friend and confidant, for help.

"We're going to follow him," my mom suggested.

"We'll wear disguises, and we'll drive in my car so he won't know it's you, and we'll find out where he's going. Then you will know, and you will know how to move forward."

Thus, the wigs.

They *did* end up doing just that—dressing up and following his car...all the way to another woman's house.

I can't imagine what my mom's friend went through that night. The moment of realization, though not totally unexpected, was undoubtedly painful. She later divorced her husband, and from what I know, she is doing okay right now, but here's the thought that keeps coming back to me about this experience: I am *so* glad she had my mom with her that night.

I don't know what my mom said to her or how she comforted her or what they talked about as they made their way back home. But I have a pretty good guess. I'm sure my mom put her arm around her friend. I'm sure she listened. I'm sure she let her friend cry, if she wanted to. And then there would have been a no-doubt-about-it, the-Lord-will-help-you kind of discussion that initially seems like it would be trite—but *never* felt anything less than heaven sent.

Total devotion. That's what my mom was willing to give.

When I was 17, I heard about a woman a few blocks away who was attacked in the middle of the night when someone entered her unlocked window. My bedroom, at the time, was at the very front of our house—far away from where my parents and siblings slept.

"Mom, my biggest fear is that I will be attacked while I sleep." I told her one evening.

"It is?" she asked—with concerned, searching eyes.

I nodded.

"Well," she replied matter-of-factly, "Then I will go get my pillow and blanket and put it right in front of your doorway. I will sleep there all night, for as long as you need me, and if anyone tries to get you, they'll have to go through *me* first."

I laughed.

I mean, *really*, we had hard wood floors. The doorway was cramped. My mom was getting "up there" in years. There was no way I would *ever* ask her to do that for me.

"I mean it," she replied. "If you are afraid to go to sleep, I just can't let that happen. I will protect you."

I still remember exactly how I felt when she said that. She was dead serious. If I had agreed, she would have slept on the hard wood floor that very night.

"It's okay, Mom," I reassured her. "I'll let you know if I need you, but I think as long as our windows and doors are locked, I'll be all right."

Fortunately, no one ever tried to break into my room, I slept just fine during the remaining years I lived at home, and my mom never had to camp in my doorway. But what mattered to me then, and what matters to me now is that she was *willing* to do it.

That total devotion, that fierce loyalty, speaks volumes.

In a world where someone rarely seems willing to give you 15 *minutes*, my mom is one of those angels who, in the appropriate circumstances, when inspired to do so, will give *everything*.

> ➤ **QUESTION:** Has a friend or family member of yours ever sacrificed a great deal for *you*? Which of those experiences means the most to you?

> ➤ **CHALLENGE:** The next time a child, family member, or friend is going through a difficult struggle, consider one way you can give of your whole self.

Lessons on Living

Hammering Candy on the Sidewalk

What do you do when your life is full of stop-gaps?

When I turned six, I had a birthday party at my house with my friends. Mom let me choose a shape out of the "cut-out cake book," and I selected the rocking horse.

The morning of the party came, and the cake was all baked, ready to be sliced, organized into that magical shape, and decorated. (Seriously, this was my favorite.)

Before we got too far along into the process, however, we realized that we didn't have any of the candies featured in the picture from the book. No lifesavers or licorice. Nothing.

I was crestfallen.

Mom didn't pause for one moment. She immediately started looking through the cupboards and found a variety of hard candies (probably more than a year old and *not* the shape of the ones in the pictures), and she said, "Oh, these will be so nice. I'll show you!"

She unwrapped the candies, placed them into a gallon-sized plastic bag, grabbed a hammer from a drawer near the window, and led me outside to the sidewalk. I warily followed.

There she proceeded to hammer those candies until they turned into dust—glittery, radiant, multi-colored dust that we then sprinkled all over the cake.

It was like she'd waved a magic wand right over that rocking horse, and I couldn't have been happier.

There was no chastisement (*Honestly, April, how ungrateful are you?*) or apologies (*I'm so sorry this couldn't be better for you.*) It was simply, "Let me show you how we can figure this out using the resources we have right now."

That simple idea has served me my whole life.

For example, we didn't have a decorated nursery for *any* of the four babies we brought home from the hospital. Alia, our first, spent the first five months of her life sleeping in a stroller, which we wheeled around our one-bedroom student apartment...sometimes putting her to sleep in the living room, sometimes in the walk-in closet, sometimes in the bathroom. I always dreamed about having pastel-painted walls, a fancy bedding set for the crib, and a matching glider for middle-of-the-night feedings, but our time, money, and space always needed to go toward other things. (It turns out that our babies didn't mind!)

When my husband and I first got married, we had a 1989 Toyota Camry that was *literally* falling apart. The starter was having some struggles, and since we were always rushing to school or to work—and trying to live wisely on a student budget—we decided to tape it together using electrical tape. Every few days, the tape would wear down, so we'd apply another sticky wrap. I'll admit that I was a bit mortified at the time. *Honestly, we're TAPING our car together?* But the vehicle was otherwise generally reliable, and it was much better than riding our bikes!

These kinds of experiences have happened over and over again.

I used to roll up the waistline of Spencer's hand-me-down pajamas because they were two inches too long.

We stuck a big bowl on top of our kitchen cabinet for about two years to catch the leak from the bathtub above until we could make it a priority to get it fixed.

We strategically placed rugs over carpet snags and positioned the hole in the love seat so it would be next to the wall.

Stop-gaps are nothing to be ashamed of.

Sure, it's nice to have everything in our lives in perfect condition, but I've learned this powerful truth: stop-gaps in one area enable progress in others.

My mom actually enjoyed my birthday party because she didn't get stressed out about making the "perfect" birthday cake.

Eric and I finished our college finals while taping our Camry together.

I created a website and an online community while my son's pajamas dragged on the ground.

We read stories to our children and sang songs around the piano while the bathtub leaked into that big bowl on top of the cabinet.

Having a life full of stop-gaps is *okay*. In fact, it's *more* than okay. They're most likely helping each of us to move forward on the things that matter most.

> ➤ *QUESTION:* Does your life seem to consist of an endless stream of stop-gaps?

> ➤ *CHALLENGE:* The next time a stop-gap frustrates you, make a conscious choice to *embrace* it, *appreciate* it, and enjoy the growth in other areas that it makes possible.

CHAPTER 7

Make-Up is Cheaper than Therapy

Are mothers people, too?

I remember the first time I ran out of make-up as a new mom. On one of those rare mornings when I actually took a *shower*, I went to open my bathroom cabinet and realized there was absolutely no way I could stretch even three more days' worth out of the powder, mascara, lipstick, or eye shadow I had tucked into my little zippered pouch.

Then that somewhat-understanding, mostly-critical voice in my head reminded me of the reality of my situation: "You have no business spending money on make-up. Your budget is tight as it is. It's not like anyone sees you, anyway. Your days of feeling beautiful are over because you're a mom now. Make-up is selfish—especially the *nice* kind of make-up. Just get over yourself and start spending your time and money on what's *really* important."

I remember going through the motions of motherhood that morning with slumped shoulders and a heavy heart. I know that probably sounds ridiculous. It was one of those "first world" problems that ultimately *isn't* a huge deal, but as a brand new mom in a new city with a busy husband and a vacant apartment complex that was my *world* each day from 6am to 6pm, it wasn't just about the make-up.

After getting Alia settled for her morning nap, I remember picking up the phone to call my mom. We chatted for a bit, and then I casually mentioned the subject of my make-up situation.

Not wanting to sound whiney, I simply said, "I can just go pick up a couple of inexpensive items from the grocery store. I don't really need nice make-up anymore."

My mom was all about simplicity. We shopped sales, and we *rarely* went to department stores. She taught me to be totally okay with whatever budget I had, and if you looked up "big spender" in a thesaurus, the antonym would be my mom.

I thought she'd agree with me and say, "April, it doesn't matter what you look like. It's what is on the inside that counts."

Then I figured she would tell me I was being kind of silly to want high-quality cosmetics. I mean, really, I had nowhere to go during the day, and no one was going to see me except my colicky baby. Add to that the fact that I'd just gotten a bad haircut at the strip mall down the street (because I didn't want to spend money at a salon), and it was perfectly clear that putting in extra resources to feel pretty just wasn't a *necessity* for me anymore.

Maybe all those things are true, and maybe under different circumstances, I would have been totally okay with that advice. But as I spoke to my mom through that phone, she could hear something deeper coming out of my heart.

It was as though I was saying, "Mothers don't need to feel beautiful. Mothers don't really matter to anyone."

And that attitude was starting to carry itself into other areas of my life: "I don't need to take care of my body. I don't need to do anything fun. It isn't important for me to invest in my mind…or go on a walk by myself, or use the bathroom without an audience. I'll be okay. Those things aren't for *me* anymore."

My mom could sense *all* of this, and she wisely said something that has stuck with me ever since.

"April, you are a queen, and you deserve the *best* make-up. If spending some extra money on cosmetics will give you a lift every single day, then by all means, go and do it! You could pay a psychologist $100 an hour to help you be happy…or you could go buy some make-up and take care of that yourself!"

That made me laugh.

I knew she was right.

We chatted for a few more minutes and said our goodbyes. Then I ended the call and sat silently for a while, holding the phone in my hands and thinking about our conversation.

I remember the powerful feeling that came over me at that point—a deep resolve being planted in my heart. It wasn't a "once and for all" kind of thing (because to this day, I still struggle with putting myself as a top priority), but that was the very first time the voice in my head acknowledged that our individual needs *matter*.

Thinking back, I can now see evidences of how my mom truly *lived* that principle:

My sister and I would play in the children's area at the YMCA while she played racquetball with her friends each week.

Occasionally she would exercise at home and blast the song, "Mony, Mony," while we did aerobics up and down the hallway, like a little parade.

She and my dad would get all dressed up to go to a fancy theater in Los Angeles a few times a year, and I always loved the smell of her perfume and the sparkle of her earrings as she kissed us goodbye.

Sometimes after dinner, she would put on a beautiful red robe, touch up her make-up, and brush her hair nicely. I would ask, "Where are you going?" or "Is someone coming over?" and she would reply, "I just want to look nice for my family."

It was normal to see stacks of books, numerous religious texts, and a collection of highlighters around the house, and sometimes Mom would slip out to her "office" to think—which was actually just the car parked in front of our house, with the driver's seat moved *all* the way back so she had plenty of room to spread her books and journals onto her lap.

I loved looking through her photo albums from her month-long excursion to China and hearing all the stories about the London trip she took with her friend, LuAnne.

And if she'd had a long day and needed to rest, she'd go right into her bed and fall asleep...no questions asked.

There were no apologies. No guilt. No worries that she wasn't giving every ounce of herself to parenthood. We felt her love and gave her the highest respect—because she showed us that parents are *people*, too.

Sometimes I wonder why I didn't "get" that as a new mom.

Sometimes I wonder why I *still* worry about taking time for myself (even sitting by myself to write this feels a little scandalous!).

Whatever the reason, I'd like to invite parents worldwide to join me and say to our families, in essence, "Because I want to do a great job taking care of *you*, I'm going to make it a priority to take care of *myself*." And whether it's makeup, an evening out, or simply an hour curled up in a comfy chair with a book that's just for *you*, it's a fantastic idea to create your own therapy.

> ➤ *QUESTION:* Do you ever have the same kinds of feelings I had about your worth as a mother? Is there something you aren't doing right now because you don't think you deserve the time, energy, or resources?

> ➤ *CHALLENGE:* Take a step back and really look at what your actions, habits, and choices are saying to your children. If there's

room for improvement, identify one thing you could do right now and do so.

CHAPTER 8

Crisis Plus Time Equals Humor

Why is it important to laugh now?

Crisis + Time = Humor

That was something I learned early on in life.

My mom was an expert with that equation, because as a mother of eight, there were a *lot* of crises.

One of my sisters knocked out her two front teeth...twice.

My then five-year-old brother once tried to use a gallon can of honey as a step stool, but ended up breaking through the plastic lid and dipping his entire foot (complete with his dirty sock) deep into the gooey sweetness.

Another sister, during an early-morning driving lesson, plunged the car into a neighbor's bush, completely destroying our radiator (and the bush).

As I returned a half-dozen eggs to a neighbor one day, holding the bag carefully and repeating in my mind my mother's instructions to carry them *carefully*, I banged the bag into a gate and dropped them all.

That's the story of family life, right?

But mom never worried about those kinds of things. Sure, she'd give us "that look" and say something like, "*Honestly...*" but we were always reminded that one day those experiences would be funny.

And now they are.

One of my favorite pieces of advice from my mother was to *never take three children grocery shopping.*

It was a rule my mother swore she would keep, but inevitably, my sister Page, my brother Ryan, and I would join my mom at Lucky Market as she tried to fill our cart with food for the week—always looking closely at the "key buy" sales.

We didn't know we were awful, but we would ask to buy *everything* that looked exciting (Fruit Loops were my favorite), and while my mom carefully evaluated the prices at the check-out, we pestered her with questions (typically about the Twix bars and Tic Tacs lining the aisle). This consistently left her exhausted by the time we got our bags of food out to the car.

I remember at least a dozen occasions when she raised her right hand— as though she were taking an oath, and said, "I will *never* take three children grocery shopping again."

We kept very serious faces because we could almost see the steam coming out of her ears, but once Mom completed her oath, my siblings and I shared knowing glances and tried to cover our smiles—because we knew there'd come a point when she wouldn't have a choice. and we'd all be back at the store together.

Sweet justice came to me, however, once *I* became a mom.

One afternoon, when my husband was in his second year of graduate school in Boston, and I was tending our three preschoolers in our little apartment, I thought it would be fun to go to a special store called "The Christmas Tree Shop." It had all kinds of toys, home supplies, and decor (year round), and I was feeling up for an adventure.

I got Alia, Grace, and Ethan bundled into their coats, hats, and mittens, got all three of them strapped into their car seats, and drove for 30 minutes to get to the shop.

Ethan began to fuss once we reached the store, so I put him in a front pack I'd brought, draped a blanket over us, and let him nurse while I pushed the cart. (In hind sight, that seems incredibly awkward, but desperate times....)

After shopping for 20 minutes, my cart was about half full, and I felt pretty excited about my purchases: a Dora tent for the girls, some lace curtains for our windows, a night light for Alia's bedroom, and a few little knick knacks to add color to our little home.

"Mommy, I have to go to the bathroom *right now*." Alia said.

"Just a few more minutes honey. I'm almost done shopping."

She started dancing. "Now, Mommy, now! I can't wait!"

More dancing. More panic in her voice. (Turns out she had contracted a strange virus, and her tummy was totally unsettled.)

I rolled the cart over to the restrooms at the back corner of the store, parked it to the right of the ladies' room door, lifted one-year-old Grace out of the cart, and proceeded to walk my two girls into a large stall in the restroom (while still nursing Ethan).

Alia needed some extra time to take care of things–more than Grace could handle–so Grace slipped under the door and started running around the empty restroom.

Splash . . . Splash . . . SPLASH!

Suddenly I realized that little Grace was running into each of the other stalls and sticking her hands into the toilets (having a *grand* old time).

I opened the door to Alia's stall so I could reign Grace back in, and Alia started screaming that someone was going to SEE her. Fortunately, no one else had come in, so I was able to grab Grace, direct her back into the stall, help Alia get cleaned up, get everyone's hands washed (especially

Grace's), and then calmly exit the restroom (though inside my head I wanted to scream).

I had spent so long in the restroom, however, that by the time I was ready to head to the check-out, the dutiful employees of The Christmas Tree Shop had re-shelved everything in my cart.

Isn't that a fun story?

It makes me laugh now. (Didn't then.)

See? Crisis plus time equals humor.

I think I'm finally learning to laugh *now*, and that's especially helpful as my mother progresses through her Alzheimer's.

This is one of my favorite stories:

When the Alzheimer's really started manifesting itself, Mom began to fall down repeatedly. She fell out of her bed, fell when she was getting up from the couch, fell in the restroom, etc. We were obviously worried for her.

One day, my sister Susan called the house to say hello and see how things were going.

Mom answered the phone with her *extra* cheerful, enthusiastic voice. "Hello?"

After the normal pleasantries, Susan asked, "Is Dad there?"

"Um, I think he's playing racquetball," my mom replied casually—a little bit confused.

Startled, because my mom wasn't to be left alone, Susan responded, "What? He's playing *racquetball?*"

"Well," Mom thought, "Maybe he's taking a nap. Or maybe he's outside watering. I'll go check!"

Knowing that if Mom stood up alone, she was likely to fall, Susan quickly said, "No! Don't go check. Why don't you just hang up the phone, and I'll call back. You let it ring so Dad can hear it, okay?"

"Oh, okay!" Mom said cheerfully.

Susan redialed the number, but as soon as the phone rang once, Mom picked it up with the same enthusiasm as the first time:

"Hello!"

"Mom," Susan reprimanded, "Don't pick up the phone. I want it to ring a few times so Dad will hear it. Just hang it up, and I'll call back. Don't pick it up."

"Oh, okay," Mom replied—this time totally convincing Susan she would be obedient.

Susan dialed the number again.

"Hello!" Mom answered after the first ring.

"MOM!" Susan said. "I am trying to get a hold of *Dad*. Don't answer the phone, okay?"

"Okay!" Mom responded cheerfully.

Five times this happened. And every single time, Mom answered the phone with the exact same enthusiasm...and absolutely no idea what was going on.

Finally, Susan stopped trying to call back and just stayed on the phone as long as she could to make sure Mom didn't try to stand up and go anywhere. (My dad wasn't far...he came into the room before too long.)

That story cracks me up every time I think about it.

Recently, I was walking through the grocery store with my children, and they asked, "Mom, why are you smiling?"

"Oh, I'm just thinking about that time Grandma kept answering the phone when Susan was trying to get a hold of Dad."

Honestly, I can't even type this without laughing. But isn't that a blessing? To be able to see the humor when life in general feels anything but funny?

This one simple skill can totally change your life, and I learned it first from my ever-patient mother, who walked through the chaos of raising eight children with missing front teeth, honey-covered socks, and an abundance of stories that we still laugh about to this day.

> ➤ *QUESTION:* What do you think would change for you if you started laughing *now* instead of later? (Of course, you can do both!)

> ➤ *CHALLENGE:* Take a minute and write down a few of the funniest stories from *your* family. Then share those stories with your family tonight at dinner—or while you're driving in the car— or while you're doing the dishes together. (And watch what happens...)

CHAPTER 9

The FTD List

What do you do when you make mistakes?

At the back of each of my mom's journals (she had a *lot* of journals throughout the years), she kept a special page labeled, "FTD." A little strange, I know, but it meant, "Fool Things I've Done."

She never specifically *showed* us her list, but she talked about it all the time—whenever something didn't go as planned or whenever she felt upset, embarrassed, or flustered. I often heard her exclaim, "This is going on my FTD list!"

Her "foolishness" wasn't that big of a deal, from my perspective. It was something like forgetting to get the tires fixed before going on a long trip—and watching them explode in front of the house *right* before we were all about to leave. The FTD list was used when a wrong substitution went into a new recipe—or when Mom forgot to note where she parked the car when we were out at a huge shopping center for the day. The FTD list was also the perfect place to report on the days when she "tried to do too much" or when she ate too many treats at a party. (*Why didn't I brush my teeth before I left the house?* I remember her saying.)

Here's what I love about that list:

1. No mistake was a waste. Every experience—no matter how frustrating—was a learning opportunity.

2. The list gave us all permission to be human. Although she never spelled it out for us, I figured that if my mom was allowed to mess up once in awhile, so was I.

3. It created an actual *system* for recognizing and remembering improvements that needed to be made. While she wasn't going to sit there and dwell on the past, she was certainly going to make sure she made better choices in the future.

Having learned from my mother's wise example, I, too, keep an FTD list in the back of my journal. Do you want to hear what's on *mine*?

Here are a few examples I'm not too embarrassed to record:

1. Instead of calmly saying to my family, "I am tired. I am going to take a nap," I started crying and yelling and running around the house, picking up the mess like a crazy lady. Somewhere in there, I think I also told my husband that everything wrong in my life was his fault. Yeah, that wasn't my best moment.

2. I spent a whole morning fretting over the dust on the furniture and thinking about how our house needed a major "reset" button—including new furniture, new paint, new art for the walls, and new carpet. Then I saw a friend's update on one of my social media accounts—where she let all of us know that her daughter, who had been struggling with health problems her whole life—was dying. Wow, did that bring life into perspective.

3. One morning, shortly after Eric started working from home, he and I were sitting at our desk together, completing a variety of computer tasks. I'm more of an introvert, and I like to work in absolute silence. Eric thrives on conversation and being around people. (Figuring out how to work together each day was a bit tricky.) After booking a flight for one of his consulting jobs, he said, "I chose seat 22A."

Wondering why on earth he needed to interrupt my train of thought to share that minor detail, I kind of let him have it. "Seriously, Eric? I'm trying to get some work done. Did you have to tell me that *right now?* Do I really need to know where you'll be sitting on the airplane?"

He paused for a moment, debating whether or not to say anything further. Finally he said this:

"I chose 22 because it's your favorite number, and I chose 'A' for April."

Oh my goodness. I can't even tell you how much I needed the FTD list at that point. *What was wrong with me?*

I will say, however, that simply writing these things down has had a profound effect on my life. I've been much more calm with my family lately, and I let them know when I'm tired (without letting that crazy lady come back...very often). I don't really worry about the dust or the thread-bare couch or the old green carpet in my bedroom. We'll fix those things when we can.

My mother showed me that it is entirely okay to make mistakes. We assess them, we learn from them, and then we keep moving forward.

(Now whenever I book a flight, I pick "21E" because 21 is Eric's favorite number....)

> ➤ **QUESTION:** So how about you? Would you benefit from an FTD list? (My mom would be excited for you!)

> ➤ **CHALLENGE:** Create a paper or digital list titled "FTD," and next time you mentally start to get after yourself, record the foolish thing you did on your list, choose to learn from your mistakes, and decide to do better next time.

CHAPTER 10

Did I Ever Tell You About My Free Cookbook?

When is it right to speak up?

Sometimes when my mom was sitting around the table with us or driving to appointments, or relaxing on the couch before bedtime, she would retell our favorite stories. Instead of fairytales, she would share our favorite family experiences over and over again.

I still remember the excitement in her voice when she launched into one of my favorite stories by saying, "Did I ever tell you about my free cookbook?"

Essentially, this is it:

One afternoon, somewhere in the 1960s or 70s (back in the era when door-to-door salesman were common), a man knocked at our door and said to my mother, "Would you like a free cookbook?"

"Free?" my mom asked warily.

"Absolutely free," he responded.

"I don't have to buy anything?" she asked.

"Not a thing."

"Well…okay. Thanks!" she responded.

The man handed her the cookbook, and then she asked him to wait just a moment while she went inside the house and put it in the kitchen. After returning to the door, with an expectant smile indicating, "What next?" the salesman started into his spiel—telling her *all* about some product or another that he wanted her to buy.

"Thank you for the information," she responded, "but I'm really not interested."

He paused for a moment, a little let down, but undoubtedly used to that response, and then said (in a slightly annoyed voice), "Okay, well, can I at least have my cookbook back?"

"*Your* cookbook?" my mom questioned. "It's *my* cookbook."

"Well, you know…. I was hoping that you would buy something from me, and I don't have a lot of those books to give away, and I've really got to make some sales today." Then sounding even *more* annoyed, he said, "Can you just give me back my book?"

Now this is when the wheels must have started turning furiously in my mother's head. She is a *nice* lady—one of the nicest you'll ever meet. I'm sure the last thing she wanted to do was hurt this man's feelings or make him look bad in front of his boss. But there's another side of my mom that I have come to appreciate more and more throughout my life. And this is the side that shows that she is *not* a doormat.

Seeing that the salesman wouldn't leave her front porch, yet being unwilling to even *consider* giving him back the cookbook that he said was hers, she quietly replied, "Just one moment," and shut the door.

He waited on that porch for a minute or two…and then another couple of minutes. *Finally* my mom came back—except she wasn't holding the cookbook. She was holding the *phone*.

"Excuse me, but I have the Better Business Bureau on the phone, and they would like to speak with you," she said.

I don't know why I always giggle during this part of the story. The words "sweet justice" keep going through my mind as I picture the expression that must have been on the salesman's face when he took the call.

My mom only heard his side of the conversation, but she watched the man as he listened intently to the bureau representative. She heard him repeatedly reply with a soft, "Mmm-hmmm." And then he hung up the phone, told my mom to enjoy her cookbook, and went on his way.

Whenever my mom told this story, it was accompanied with bright eyes and a big smile. She was proud of herself—not for turning a salesman away, but for teaching him an important lesson about honesty and hopefully saving a handful of her neighbors from getting swindled.

What did this teach me?

You can be kind, but still prove a point and insist on integrity. It's common today to yell and scream to get your way. (I worked a customer service job in college, and wow...), but I've never felt the need to do that because I saw the way my mom modeled these necessary exchanges. Being firm and being kind are not mutually exclusive.

Another example of this was when my mom and I went to visit my grandma (her mom) at a local care facility for the elderly. I can't remember all the details, but Grandma had been checked into this new hospital-looking place, and we dropped in to see how things were going.

What we saw pierced our hearts.

Grandma was in her 90s, going a bit senile, and she yelled a lot during the day and night (sometimes she sang really loud, and sometimes she unapologetically swore...). Well, the staff didn't like that because it bothered the other residents, so they gave her heavy doses of drugs, which kept her quiet and slumped in her wheelchair.

Then we noticed bandages on both of her forearms and discovered that her delicate skin had been torn during her diaper changes (she wasn't cooperative, and the staff members were too rough).

I remember watching my mom as she studied her mother's condition. I remember hearing her ask a steady stream of follow-up questions to the (quickly-backpedalling) staff on call.   And then I watched her make it *perfectly* clear that this was absolutely unacceptable and that she was taking her mother home the very next day.

There was no screaming. No blaming. No unkind words. But as I saw the fire in her eyes and heard the unwavering declaration that *this was not to ever* happen again, I thought, "*Go* Mom."

Another thing I learned is that we *have* to stand up for ourselves—and our families. This part is hard for me because I am my father's daughter. He'd rather pay $40 for a jar of peanut butter than have to confront the cashier about the mistaken charge.   However, to live and work and interact within our society, this skill of speaking up and standing tall really isn't an option.

That's why we go to bat for political measures that shape our society. That's why we call our elementary school teacher when she shows a way-to-scary PG-13 movie to her class. That's why we get on the phone with the insurance company that is clearly robbing its customers.

We can be respectful and kind, but if we, as parents who guard the home and family, don't stand up for what's good and right, *who will?*

It's also now clear to me that our voices mean something. I don't know if you're like me, but I have a tendency to underestimate my influence. I'll think, "What do I really have to contribute?" or "No one's going to want to hear my take on things." But what I've learned is that you cannot *not* influence other people. Who we are, what we say, and how we say it has a powerful influence everywhere we go.

Your experiences—good and bad—have prepared you to now strengthen others and improve your community. Your understanding of what is right is essential to the global conversations going on, and everywhere you turn, there are people who desperately need what you have to offer. Sure, that sounds a bit grandiose, but sit still for a minute and think about that. You'll know it's true.

I'm guessing you're going to have an opportunity (or two or three) this week to really use your voice. Maybe you'll have the chance to intervene in a heated discussion, maybe you'll feel inspired to stand against a bully, or maybe you'll be promoting a cause you know to be right.

Is this easy? Is it comfortable? Is it how we would choose to spend our time?

Most of the time, no.

But this is what we do. This is how we strengthen our societies and teach our children to do the same, and I'm so grateful that my mother taught me this lesson when I was young, through something as simple as a free cookbook.

> ➤ **QUESTION:** How have you shown your children the importance of using your voice? What helps you to do so in a way that models appropriate behavior for your children?

> ➤ **CHALLENGE:** The next time something happens that makes your blood boil, stop for a moment and consider the possibility of responding with a firm, kind, unwavering voice.

Lessons on Parenthood

CHAPTER 11

Purse Compartments and Sorting Socks

What are the little things that bring us together?

"Ooh! What do you think of this one?" I held up a cute yellow purse that had been hanging on a rack at one of our local department stores.

"Darling!" My mom replied. "But I have to see the *compartments*," she smiled.

"Well, of course!" I replied with a laugh. Because if a purse doesn't have a variety of compartments inside, it might as well be a grocery sack. That idea had been ingrained in me from the time I could drape a purse strap over my shoulder and wobble around the house wearing my mom's high-heeled shoes.

But it wasn't just *using* the compartments that made my mom happy (though she adored the fact that she could have a separate place for her checkbook, lipstick, tissues, keys, and receipts). She mostly enjoyed sharing the *joy* of the compartments with the people she loved...namely, us.

One of my favorite stories told by three of my older sisters was how my mom would buy a new purse at a bargain price (it was *always* at a bargain price), and then stop by each of my sisters' places on the way home—to take them on a tour of her new treasure.

I love to imagine her knocking at each door: "Hi Laura/Lisa/Susan! I was just on my way home from buying a new purse!"

Then, because they knew her so well and because this kind of thing happened so often, they would say, "How fun! Can you show me the compartments?'

Once my mom entered their homes, they must have sat down close to each other on the couch while she went through each snap and zipper.

But after that, the conversation would have changed to focus on each one of *them*.

> *How are you doing today? Is there anything concerning you? Can I do any-thing to help?*

I know because that's what she did for me.

I remember coming home from drama rehearsal or cheer practice and finding my mom on the couch "switching handbags." Her eyes would light up as she saw me, and I would say something like, "Is that a new purse?"

"Yes!" she would exclaim. "Let me show you!"

To be honest, I didn't share the same excitement, but I would humor her and try not to laugh as she enthusiastically walked through each and every pocket—sharing ideas about which was best-suited for what.

Certainly, this process was something she adored, but looking back, I can see what it *really* did for us. It brought me—her teenage daughter going through all the craziness of high school—to her side, in an environment where I could open up about *anything*.

I don't know exactly how she did it, but once the purse discussion ended, we simply kept talking. I can't even remember all the conversations, but I remember what I *felt*: safe, happy, loved, and lucky to be hers.

Thinking more deeply about this, I realize this didn't only happen with purses. It also happened with *socks*.

My sister Susan had four boys in rapid succession, and the number of socks that needed to be washed each week was enormous. Susan detested sorting the socks—trying to figure out whose were whose, so as often as possible, when we were driving by Susan's house on the way home from the orthodontist or something like that, Mom would say, "Why don't we drop by and see if we can help sort the boys' socks?"

I remember sitting cross-legged on the floor of Susan's living room, a huge laundry basket of socks in the center, and the three of us making matches and rolling sock balls while Susan's boys ran around us, playing with their toys.

"I just keep all the socks here in this basket," Susan told me one day, "and if I need socks for the boys, I just search in here for a pair...until Mom comes by, and we sort them together. It makes it more fun."

I agreed. Our sock-folding talks were my favorite because Susan always asked me about my latest crush or my activities in school, and I was consistently ready to talk all about it.

One afternoon, once I had become a mother and moved away from my hometown, I attended a class about managing housework. A lady in the back of the room raised her hand and said, "If you get a mesh bag for each child in the family, you can keep everyone's socks separate. Then you just throw the bag in the washing machine, and you never have to sort socks again!"

What? Never sort socks again? No more conversations around Susan's laundry pile? No more laughing while we worked and then hugging each other tightly before we left?

Now, clearly, I know there are benefits to being efficient. There's always plenty of work to do, and relationship-building doesn't have to stop just because we figure out a faster way to do our housework, but when I tried to identify why the idea of mesh bags bothered me so much, I understood that these little traditions of sharing purse compartments and folding socks served the beautiful purpose of bringing my family together.

Take a moment and go through this exercise with me. Can you think of something that seems totally inconsequential or unsophisticated, but it brings you physically and emotionally closer to the ones you love?

Here are a couple of examples:

My husband and I have just a few small boxes of Christmas decorations. Neither one of us likes to shop or decorate, and we'd much rather spend our money on books or travel. So while we might add a thing or two to our holiday collection each year, it's *nothing* like what we see in the neighbors' yards around us (working ferris wheels, fancy train sets, lighted villages...). One Christmas, when our budget was particularly tight and our workload felt particularly heavy, Grace came out to the garage with me to hold the step stool in place while I reached for our boxes.

As I set the first box on the ground, I thought, "Man, all I have is a bunch of junk. I don't have anything nice to decorate our home."

But when we opened it, Grace squealed, "MEMORIES!!!" and immediately started taking out each little item as though it were a treasure...because to her, that's exactly what it was.

Ethan, my first son/third child, loves to sing, and he has a knack for picking out harmonies. That skill simply came with him, and sometimes when we drive, we'll turn on a song we love and belt it out at the top of our lungs—me singing the melody, Ethan finding the perfect alto or tenor part to go with it.

One afternoon, with the two of us alone in the car driving to pick up some groceries, I let him buy a new Owl City song on my iPhone. We sang together the whole way to the store, but when it was time to get out of the car and start our shopping, he asked, "Can we listen to it again and again and again?"

My first instinct was to hurry into the store and pick up the singing on the way home. I was tired, and I wanted to get my errands done as quickly as possible.

But looking at the excitement in his eyes and realizing that I wouldn't always have a 10-year-old son with me, I agreed.

We sat together in our parked car with the volume cranked up, singing our hearts out.

I remember thinking, "*This* is motherhood."

Although my mom doesn't know my name anymore, and although our time together is centered around her hospital bed, I still long to be with her...to hold her soft hands and hear her voice and see the love that's in her eyes. That's why I go every Thursday with my children. I bring along the ingredients to make dinner, the latest chapter of this book, and sometimes a small gift—or something my daughter has painted to hang on her wall. I'm not really *needed*, I guess. She most likely won't remember I was there, and her nurse is available to take care of all her physical needs. But *I* desperately need her. And because she always put me as a priority in *her* life, I want to show her that she's a priority in *mine*.

In fact, it was fun to see things come full circle recently when my daughter Alia purchased a new wallet. "I was so excited when it came in the mail that I took it into the office to show Dad," she told me. "I pointed out all of the different places I could store cards and money and my phone, and then I realized I was just like Grandma—showing him all my compartments!"

Learning to bind our hearts to our children's—and their hearts to ours—isn't something we're taught in a prenatal class or at a parenting conference. It's not even something you *notice* while it's happening, and it's typically surrounded by a series of not-so-enjoyable events. (For example, while I was writing this chapter, two children were bickering about the blanket fort they built in the garage, and another child got upset with them for assuming that the 12 stuffed animals the said child put in their closet four months ago were actually theirs to *keep*.)

But when I assess my time with my children—considering all our imperfections and the many ways we frustrate each other—I'm learning to look a little deeper and place the most value on the seemingly insignificant experiences that are, in fact, bringing us together.

➤ *QUESTION:* What are the little moments in your life that bring you and your children together?

➤ *CHALLENGE:* Take a moment to assess the strength of your relationships, and the next time an opportunity comes up to do something "little" that will set the stage for conversation and physical closeness, *do it.*

CHAPTER 12

Painting the Bread and Silly Putty Messages

What will our children remember?

Homemade bread was a staple in our home growing up. I remember walking into the house after school on "bread day," and Mom would have timed it *just* right so her bread was fresh out of the oven. We liked to "paint" the loaves with melted butter and then eat thick slices covered with honey.

The bread was only part of the magic, though. What I *really* loved was sitting in the warm kitchen next to my mom while she asked me about my day. She never pressured me to talk, but she was 100 percent available— just in case I wanted to open up about my friends, my latest book report, or any recent conversations that had troubled me.

Some days were busier than others, and she wasn't sitting in the kitchen with homemade bread *every day*, but I knew there would always be a pocket of time when we could sit together and share our hearts.

Now before you start worrying about how your life is too busy for bread baking or giving uninterrupted quality time to each of your family members, let's back up for a moment. I'm in the same boat. My life and responsibilities are not the same as my mother's. I move at a different pace. I have different strengths.

That's okay.

The point of this chapter isn't to make you *or* me feel like we're failing.

The point is to identify what it is that our children will *remember* so we can invest in those things. Make sense?

I'm sure my mom didn't go to bed each night patting herself on the back for all the quality time she spent with us. She worried about her weight and her messy bedroom. She got nervous before teaching a lesson at church. And there were always piles of papers that needed to be sorted—bills to pay, investment newsletters to read, and social invitations to coordinate and put on the calendar. My grandmother lived with us for five years, and my mom was her primary caregiver...demonstrating a beautiful love that I still remember to this day.

In the midst of all of my mother's many responsibilities, however, there were special moments when it was "just us."

Everyone has discretionary family time that pops up throughout the day. The question is simply, "What do we *do* with that time?"

To help answer that question, I'd like to take you back in time to my parents' 50th wedding anniversary.

The entire extended family (all eight of their children and their spouses—plus most of the grandchildren) gathered in my little backyard on that special evening, and my siblings and I took turns reading from a "memory list" we had created in anticipation of the event.

I kept a copy, and I think you'll be interested in hearing a few of the things we recorded:

- Driving back from Tijuana in the VW bus and running out of gas. Cousin Beth played songs on the new guitar we bought for about $10.00 and we all sang along with her until Dad came back.

- Mom praying for us whenever we had a test at school. She'd say, "Now what time is your test?" Then once we would tell her, she would say, "I will set my alarm, and right when you're taking your test, I will be praying for you."

- Mowing the dead lawn with Dad. I don't think we ever had green grass.

- Eating cake and ice cream around the ping-pong table for birthdays (Thanksgiving too).

- Taking family trips to the tide pools.

- When I would wake in the night I would go right to Dad and squeeze next to him because Mom would make us lay on the floor.

- Peeking at the Christmas presents in their closet or along the wall in their room, with just a blanket over them.

- Watching home movies recorded on filmstrips—that would burn every time because the projector got too hot. Dad would say, "Oh, my achin' back!"

- Taking naps in the afternoon and getting a sliced apple in a little red bowl before we settled down.

- Coming home from school on rainy days (all soaking wet) to popcorn and hot chocolate ready to eat by the heater to keep us warm.

- Going to Fedco and singing songs in the bus. Then buying treats at the end of our shopping trip.

- Family Nights in the back room of the Blue House. Mom would play the piano, we would all sing, and I felt like I was in heaven.

- Going roller-skating with Mom one time. I was nine, and I had no clue she could skate! I think Mom only kept her skates on for ten minutes, and Dad walked next to her most of the time, holding onto her arm so she wouldn't fall.

- Looking through all of the photo albums Dad put together.

- Driving me on my paper route when it rained.

- Sharing spiritual experiences and feeling as if they really understood what I was feeling.

- Fourth of July Block Parties...we would decorate our bikes in the morning for the parade and then have a great time eating and playing with our friends.

- Asking if I was waiting for "the slave" to take my clothes up to my bedroom.

- Always walking in on Mom or Dad praying next to their bed. This happened often, and one of the reasons I have such confidence in prayer today is because I saw them doing it consistently.

- Many mornings when getting ready for school, we'd ask what the weather report was. Mom would say, "Yucka bean, yucka stew, the weather report is 72."

- They always had time for me.

- Mom would try to clean out her nightstand drawer or her purse, and I would always find her at that time. I would always want to touch her "fun" stuff and she would say, "Quiet Hands."

- On my lunch sack for school, mom would always write my name so beautifully, along with a perfect happy face. I just loved it!

- Blue Moon. Mom's signature song she always played on the piano.

- Dad singing, "Granada" really loud.

- I remember asking Mom, while she was making dinner in the kitchen, if I could help her make it. She said I could help her by going outside. (That's why I don't spend much time in the kitchen now!)

- The many drives into San Clemente to see my eye doctor, Dr. Farr. And boy, was it FAR to drive! It seemed like forever! And mom would do that for me.

- I loved my stuffed dog, Thessalonian, that she bought me before going into the hospital for an eye operation.

- Devotionals before school each morning. She would take the time to read the scriptures and pray with us every day before school. We each had our own scriptures, ruler, and pencil - red lead on one side and blue on the other.

- We loved our Garage Sale Christmas presents almost as much as the new gifts! Really, we did.

- Every Saturday before we could play, we would have to pick up all the leaves in front from the rubber tree.

- Playing chess late at night.

- Hiding candy from me.

- Receiving a handwritten letter every week for two years while I served a mission for church.

- Helping us with our school projects.

- I would be hanging out with friends in my room, and it would be around 1:00 A.M. and Mom would come in the room asking if we would like her to bake some cookies for us to eat.

- I was invited to go see a questionable movie with my friends, and Mom offered to take me shopping instead so I wouldn't go see the movie. She took me over to Marina Pacifica, and we chose a wooden dollhouse that you had to paint and put together. I loved shopping with mom since we didn't seem to do it nearly enough (as far as I was concerned), and I really enjoyed the one-on-one time together. I felt special and had a great time and was glad I didn't go to the movies. I don't think we ever finished that dollhouse but the memory has stayed with me.

- Doing the Macarena on the sidewalk as we drove away from the house.

- Every note was signed with "XOXOXOXOXOXO." I loved that.

- Mom scraping off offensive bumper stickers (yes, from *other people's* cars).

- Going to the library and reading Family Circus cartoon books on the lawn, sharing the funny ones.

- Mom picked me up from school one day and took me to see *The Burb's* with Tom Hanks at the movie theater. When I asked her why, she said just because she wanted to spend some time with me.

- Listening to and comforting me when I was sad that I didn't have a best friend or felt like a third wheel.

- Mom and Dad always showed us how to live by their examples. They practiced what they preached and taught.

Do you notice the same things that I noticed? The memories recorded had very little to do with how much money was spent or how "grand" the event was. The focus is on how these activities *felt*. Each of us wants to know that we *matter*. It's that *feeling* we remember.

It's been fun watching my husband create beautiful memories for our children. (I'm not as natural at that as he is.) One night we heard there was going to be a meteor shower—and the best time to watch it was somewhere between midnight and 2am. I was exhausted from a busy day of mothering, and there was no way I was going to get up *on purpose* in the middle of the night, but Eric was excited to create an experience for our children. When the twilight hours came, he woke up each child, drove them in their pajamas up the hill to a local park, and created a bed in the back of his truck where they could lie down and watch the heavens.

They couldn't wait to "report" to me in the morning.

I personally had an eye-opening experience a few years ago when my daughter Grace was planning the games for her birthday party.

She thought it would be fun to survey her friends, so she wrote up 8-10 questions and titled the page, "How well do you know Grace?"

I looked through the questions as she was making photocopies, and I was pricked in the heart as I realized I didn't know the answer to *any* of the questions:

- What's Grace's shoe size?

- What is she afraid of?

- What is her favorite subject in school?

Yes, I knew she liked pandas and having her nails painted and getting back tickles, but I couldn't answer the questions that were important to *her*.

We had a good talk that morning, and she brought me totally up to speed, but that was a wake-up call for me to pay closer attention to the *little* things.

This is a journal entry from a few years ago, when I more fully came to understand the power of small moments:

> *This morning was full of trouble making. Spencer drank out of the gutter and then colored with dry erase marker all over his door and the living room wall.... But in spite of the inevitable chaos, the day turned out to be one of my favorites.*
>
> *Tonight we gathered in the family room after dinner and listened to some of our favorite music. Eric has a passion for singing in harmony, so he started teaching our three oldest children how to pick out different parts, and we sang for nearly two hours—stopping occasionally to remember a funny story related to one of the songs or to break out some new dance moves.*

As we were singing our new "Perry Family Theme Song" tonight, my husband and I just looked at each other—both of us feeling the same deep emotion.

This is what we've always dreamed about. After years of hard work, it's finally happening.

Here's one more story I recorded that I call "Silly Putty and Fudge Pops":

When Ethan got home from kindergarten this morning, we ate lunch together and then started to play with some new silly putty we bought last week. I knew you could use silly putty to pick up the ink from a newspaper, but I didn't know it worked with penciled drawings on plain old per. Ethan and I started writing phrases to each other (backwards) and then revealing the message with the silly putty. So fun. I wrote his name, some funny notes, and finally, "Want a fudge pop?" His face lit up when he read the message, and we sat there together on the kitchen counter, swinging our legs and enjoying our dessert, giving little Spencer some bites, and laughing about all the messages we'd written on the silly putty.

It was at that moment I realized that being a mother doesn't have to be complicated. It's okay if my children don't have the latest clothes or a ton of extra activities. In a few years, shopping and after-school classes won't be as difficult for me to juggle, and perhaps we'll do more of those things. Vacations are great, and we'll make sure we have plenty of family bonding moments before our children grow up, but again, an exotic vacation isn't critical to family success. When I look at life clearly and identify what really matters, it's the love we feel inside the walls of our own home. Tomorrow I'm going to stock up on silly putty and fudge pops.

These are the kinds of things I never learned in a Parenting class. And I'm not sure I would have really *understood* the concept until I experienced it for myself. But something interesting happens to me when I reflect on stories like these. I feel less stressed. I feel more excited to be with my children. I feel less worried about doing "big" things and more interested in creating memories my children will hold forever.

I don't make bread every week, and my efforts often pale in comparison to what I *wish* they could be, but in the end, I—like you—am willing to give everything I can to make life beautiful for our children.

> ➢ **QUESTION:** What are the most cherished memories from *your* childhood? What do you want your own children to say about you someday?

> ➢ **CHALLENGE:** Take a moment to assess your current family relationships and identify one way you can more fully focus on what your children will *remember.*

CHAPTER 13

Frozen Yogurt with a Flourish

How does our love come full circle?

When I had three preschoolers, life felt overwhelming.

You understand, I'm sure.

I craved sleep, most of my wardrobe consisted of my "mom uniform" (jeans and a t-shirt) and the process of finishing a full conversation with an adult or writing down a complete thought felt like a distant memory.

I *loved* being home with my children—don't get me wrong. I didn't wish those days away, but that doesn't mean they were easy.

There were lots of phone calls to my mom during those years. I would say, "Mom, I'm having such a hard time!"

And she would say, "There, there, April. Everything will be fine. You just put your feet up on the couch as much as you can, and it's okay if you can't do everything. You're doing a great job, and the Lord is so happy with the love you are giving your children."

Those reassuring phone calls got me through the rough patches week after week, but one day, during a particularly stressful period of time, my husband could tell I needed a break. Eric arranged to take our children out for an afternoon and dropped me off for a special date with my mom (just the two of us!).

First stop was our favorite frozen yogurt place.

I was giddy with excitement. I was wearing *real clothes*. I'd put on makeup and done my hair, and just walking into a business establishment without a diaper bag felt like I was walking into a spa.

Mom and I placed our orders, and then when we sat down at our table to eat our yogurt, she said, "Now close your eyes for a minute."

"What?" I asked—totally confused.

"Close your eyes. I have a surprise."

So I closed my eyes and listened while my mom rustled around in the paper sack she'd brought with her and set some things on our table.

What on earth is she doing? I thought to myself.

Thirty seconds passed, and then a minute. Finally it was quiet, and she said, "Okay! You can open your eyes!"

There on the table were two crystal goblets and two silver spoons. She'd transferred our yogurt from the paper cups into the goblets, and, with a big smile on her face, said, "Today I am eating yogurt with a *queen*."

I wish I could accurately explain how I felt at that point.

I think I must have laughed and looked around to see if anyone in the store thought we looked ridiculous, but really, as we sat together with our goblets of yogurt, reminisced about the funny things my children had been doing, and talked about our lives and our goals and our families, I thought, "There couldn't be a more beautiful mother in the whole world."

I shared that story with my daughters a few months ago—days before we'd planned to drive into Long Beach for our regular Thursday visit, which also happened to be the week of my mother's birthday.

"Let's do this for Grandma Zoe!" my girls exclaimed. "We can pick up yogurt from the shop by Grandma's house, and we can pack our crystal goblets, and we can do the same thing for her that she did for you!"

I don't know why I didn't think of that myself, but I jumped at the opportunity. We did exactly as the girls had planned, and while my mother rested in her bed, not quite sure who we were or why we were eating frozen yogurt in goblets, I had the chance to see a mother's love come full circle.

I'm bringing this up because as I've been working on this book, and as I've been sharing these stories with my friends, I often hear this: "April, you have a *great* mom, and I love to read about your experiences with her. But what about those of us who weren't raised by a mom like that? What do you say to someone whose mother is just *mean*...or someone who has a strained relationship with their mother pretty much all the time?"

Those situations are hard. I'm not going to lie. I have no idea how my life would have turned out had I been born into a different family.

But here's my best advice: You break the cycle.

In some ways, that's what my mom did.

My grandma (we called her MeMe) was a no-nonsense kind of lady. Mom always spoke kindly of her, but not *affectionately*. MeMe worked my mom hard. She had a strong personality. She got things done, but she was never described as "gentle" or "sweet."

I only knew MeMe as a 90+-year-old woman. During the final five years of her life, my mom cared for her in our home, and these are the kinds of things I saw:

- My mom treated her mother with the most beautiful compassion you've ever seen.

- Since we had too many people in the house and not enough beds, Mom put a mat on the floor of her room for my little brother, and MeMe got the "racecar" bed next to the bunk bed my sister and I shared. (When MeMe realized, after a few months, that she had been sleeping in a racecar, she said, "If my friends at the old folks' home could see me now!")

- I watched Mom trim MeMe's nails and give her sponge baths. She served her meals on a little tray and sent us in with bowls of mint-and-chip ice cream.

- One day, MeMe poured a whole bottle of Chanel No. 5 all over her body. We had to open the windows so we could breathe. Mom kindly washed her off.

- Another day, we came home from church, and Grandma didn't have a stitch of clothing on. Mom hurried and dressed her.

- When MeMe became especially senile, she started interacting with her imaginary friends. She would hold things on her head and scream for her "friends" to take the book/spoon/bowl of ice cream. Mom would instruct us to sneak behind MeMe's chair and do as she wished.

- I ended up sleeping in the hallway for months because MeMe yelled a lot in the night and liked to sing all four verses of *Battle Hymn of the Republic.* Mom made sure I was comfortable out there.

- MeMe didn't want us to wear red because the Russians were coming. Mom just smiled and bought us red clothes anyway, assuring her mother that all would be well.

- Sometimes, MeMe swore like a sailor, and we covered our mouths with our hands and tried *really* hard not to laugh. Mom thought it was hilarious.

Years after my grandma passed away, I asked my mom if it had been stressful to care for her mother.

"No," she replied, "It was always a pleasure. I can honestly say she was never a burden."

I wish everyone had the opportunity to experience the same sweetness I felt in my home, thanks to my remarkably loving parents. I'm not sure why it doesn't work out that way. But here's what I do know: each one of us has a choice. Having a stressful home life can't " make" someone a bad parent. And even though my mom showed me how to love others nearly *perfectly,* it's still a struggle for me every single day. (Ask my husband and kids!)

The point is that you and I are *trying.* And if you don't know where to begin, let's start by remembering to treat others as queens or kings— whether it's with a goblet of frozen yogurt or an extra measure of gentleness in our daily interactions.

- **QUESTION:** If you were to continue the traditions set by your parents, what would your family become? (How do you feel about that? How are you doing, in general?)

- **CHALLENGE:** As you go throughout your days and weeks, think far into the future and consider how your actions today will shape your posterity. (If necessary, be brave enough to be the change you wish to see.)

CHAPTER 14

Jumping Up and Down Outside the Choir Room

What do our children really want to know?

My senior year of high school, there was one specific scholarship I *really* hoped to get, but of course I procrastinated writing my essays and didn't have them ready until the day before the deadline.

"Oh mom," I said, "let's just not send this in. My chance of getting this scholarship is so slim, and my essays aren't that great, and I waited too long."

But she wouldn't hear of it. She had been moved by what I had written in my essays, and—clutching my application to her chest—said, "I *must* send these in." Then she ran to the post office right before it closed, paid the overnight mailing fee, and called the scholarship office to make sure they knew my application was on its way.

I remember thinking she had wasted her money, but she looked so sure of herself that I didn't say a word other than "thanks."

A few weeks later, while I was at an after-school rehearsal for our spring musical, there was a soft, rapid knock at the choir room door. The room full of singers and dancers paused, and everyone craned their necks to see who was there.

It was my mom.

I slipped outside into the cool air, joined my mom at the top of the metal staircase where she was standing, and said, "Mom, what are you *doing* here?"

She was jumping up and down, clasping a large white envelope in her arms.

"April, it came! It came!"

I looked at the return address and saw it was the response to my scholarship application, but not wanting to get too excited, I said, "I'm sure it's just a letter telling me I didn't get it. You didn't have to come all the way down here."

She acted like she hadn't even heard me and simply thrust the envelope into my hands and watched with a huge smile on her face as I opened it.

Well, I *did* get that particular scholarship, and of course it was an exciting moment.

But as I stood there by the choir room door, listening to the muffled sounds of the rehearsal going on inside and hugging my mom as she wiped the tears from her eyes, the main thought going through my mind wasn't about the scholarship.

Instead I was thinking, "My mom really believes in me."

That is what I think each of us really wants to know—even though it might *appear* that we are ungrateful or indifferent. Deep inside, we're hopeful that someone, *somewhere* out there, believes in who we are, what we can do, and who we can become.

Think for a minute about the people in *your* life who have supported you during your best (and worst) moments.

What kind of an effort did that take for them? How did you feel as a result? What kind of a person did that inspire *you* to be?

As we're each working to become that kind of support to others, here are a couple of thoughts that may help:

1 - Our small efforts add up over time.

Like you (I'm guessing) I often feel like I'm spread too thin. Sometimes I can barely *think* at the end of the day because my brain is so tired, and then when I think back to my mom's example, I wonder, "How on earth did she do it?"

But then I look a little deeper, and I can see how my small efforts–just like *your* small efforts–start to add up.

For example, a few years ago, my girls wanted to make special photo-Valentines that made it look like they were holding the lollipops we stuck through each card. We did photo shoots out in the backyard, edited the pictures on the computer, and then ordered prints from the store. Those kinds of projects aren't "my thing" at all, but the girls were giddy with excitement.

I remember another day, when my then-four-year-old son Spencer was ooh-ing and ahh-ing over the car ads in the newspaper, so I helped him make a car dealership out of a cereal box and showed him how he could line up his Hot Wheels in the "parking lot" and put little price tags on them.

He *lit up*.

Sometimes it's just taking 10 minutes to research Lego sets online with Ethan or help my high school student memorize a passage from *Romeo and Juliet* for her Language Arts class. Other times, it's simply being available and listening intently to what another person wants to say...without glancing down at my phone or slyly checking the clock.

Those are just a few examples from *my* life, but I see these kinds of things in *your* lives all the time.

I see parents of children with special needs spend long hours (and sometimes days) in hospital rooms, doctors' offices, and therapy visits.

I sit in the back row during choir concerts and awards ceremonies and count *hundreds* of cameras flashing and recording every detail.

I read updates on social media where friends and family members cheer each other on for each advancement, celebration, or success.

By themselves, these things seem ordinary, but over a lifetime, their composite goodness is anything but.

2 - Sometimes the *most* important moments are the hardest.

I remember the one time I stayed out too late with a boy on a date. Why was it only once? Because when the boy brought me home, probably about an hour or two after I *should* have been home, my dad was standing on the sidewalk wearing his bathrobe, and he was *not* happy.

I was mortified.

I went to bed that night in tears—totally embarrassed and frustrated that I was being treated "like a child" (I was seventeen and thought I knew way more than I did...).

My dad certainly didn't enjoy waiting up for me, or sending me to bed when I was so emotional, but that night, he clearly communicated his love and concern to a teenager who was trying to "figure herself out." That single event sent a message loud and clear: He had high expectations for me and believed I could be better than I was. And because he handled that situation with such grace, I, of course, wanted to rise to the challenge.

When it was finally time for me to graduate from high school, my mom drove me over to the school for the ceremony. I remember getting out of the car, wearing my cap and gown, with medallions dangling around my neck. I began to walk toward the entrance of the auditorium, but my mom said, "Wait! I need a picture!"

"Mom," I replied, looking around at the cars parked along the curb, "This is a terrible background. Why don't we take some pictures afterward by the trees?"

"I will," she responded, "but I want to remember this very moment. Right here—while you're getting out of the car. I want to remember how beautiful you look. I am *so proud of you.*"

Of course I gave in. I remember humoring her with a smile as I stood by the trunk of our car, and throughout the next several years—until her memory went away—she would say, "Remember that time I took your picture by the car before your graduation? That was such a happy day."

There really isn't a recipe for showing another person that you care, and you may never find yourself jumping up and down outside of a choir room. But I'm hopeful that when opportunities come to interact with the people who matter deeply to us, we'll remember that what they *really* want to know is that we believe in them.

> ➤ **QUESTION:** Who are the people in your life that you want to more fully support? How can you do this in a way that will have lasting impact?

> ➤ **CHALLENGE:** Take a moment to record the times in your life when you have felt most supported. Then identify one way you can improve in your own interactions with the ones you love.

CHAPTER 15

"Mom, I Need You."

When is it time to drop everything else?

I spent a couple of days in the hospital a few years ago after a difficult surgery.

Mom had checked me in while my husband cared for our four young children at home. She made sure I came out of the anesthesia all right and then stayed by me late into the night. When I could tell she was getting sleepy, I said, "You can go home now, Mom. I'm fine. Thanks for being with me today."

But that night was *awful*. The pain was more intense than I had imagined it would be. The medicine I'd been given wasn't working, and the nurses barely responded when I pushed my call button.

I remember watching the clock carefully all night, writhing in pain and wondering when it would be the right time to call my mom. As soon as it was light, I picked up the phone.

She answered by the second ring, and then I said (in a soft voice, with hardly any energy, while trying not to burst into tears), "Mom, I *need* you."

I didn't need to say anything more. She understood, and she quickly replied, "I will be there in 20 minutes," (which she was).

Somehow she magically got the nurses to coordinate the proper pain medication, and then while I slept for pretty much the whole day, my mom sat in a chair at the foot of my bed, reading, writing in her journal, and just waiting to serve me whenever I opened my eyes.

I can't even tell you how comforted I felt—seeing her there every time I woke up.

In fact, that's what I sometimes wish I had *now*. Do you ever wake up when the house is quiet and then remember all the stressful situations you're trying to handle? Do you sometimes feel so inadequate when it comes to completing all of your responsibilities that you wish you didn't have to get out of bed?

If my mom could be right next to me every day—fighting my battles for me and taking care of my every need, a part of me would be *thrilled*. But that's not how life works, is it? There comes a point when we not only have to rise up and meet our *own* challenges, but we then become a source of strength for *others*. I don't know that we're ever ready for that transition, but I'm learning that's what happens when we grow up.

Clearly, life feels easier when we don't have to go through it alone, but let's talk about this balance for a moment. When is it time to "drop everything" and be there for those we love, and when is it best to let them become self-reliant?

I don't have "the answer," but here are some thoughts:

1 - We want to be there for as many pivotal times as possible.

When I was growing up, my parents came to all my violin concerts, school plays, and Back-to-School Nights, and I loved that, but there were some other pivotal moments that mattered to me even more.

Our seventh grade election results were accidentally botched. After two days of thinking I had won, the administrators announced that, due to an error with the ScanTron machine, all of the winners were actually losers. Mom held me in her arms when I got home from school that day. I think she was more upset than I was, but she comforted me.

I remember another night, coming home from work shortly after graduating from high school—feeling terrible about the way a co-worker had treated me. My mom was already asleep, but she woke up when I came in and listened to the whole story before offering beautiful advice that helped my mind to rest.

Some pivotal moments simply "happened" while we were chopping vegetables together or emptying the dishwasher. Those involved conversations where I was able to talk through my feelings about motherhood, college, and other major life decisions. I wouldn't trade those moments for the world.

The time we spend with one another is more valuable than we know. It might feel mundane at the time, but it *matters* when we're there.

2 - Sometimes the moments we *can't* be there will enable our loved ones to grow.

This is a very important concept that has taken me awhile to understand. I can't tell you how guilty I felt when I missed my son's sixth grade back-to-school night because my husband and I were at a conference. I've also occasionally sent my children to school with my point-and-shoot camera when I couldn't make it to an awards ceremony. *Will you ask your teacher to take your picture?*

Sometimes things come up. Sometimes our work requires travel. Sometimes we can't be there for *every single special moment*. But I've personally found that some of my most growth-producing experiences have happened when I've been on my own.

For example, my parents lived in Mexico City for 18 months while on a service mission for our church. During that time, my husband was going to school in Boston, and I delivered our third child, Ethan, 10 weeks early. While Eric went to Los Angeles to start his summer internship, our daughters stayed at his mother's home, and I stayed in Boston to tend to our baby in the NICU.

That was an *incredibly* lonely time...and I would have loved to have had my mom by my side, but because that wasn't possible, I had to develop a new strength. My mother had fortunately modeled exactly how to handle challenging situations throughout all my growing-up years, so I had the confidence that I could follow in her path.

I learned to pray hard, and I discovered I could navigate the medical system, hire movers, order groceries online, and coordinate our flights to Los Angeles once the NICU days were over. Later that summer, when our family was totally reunited, I discovered I could keep a three-year-old and a one-year-old occupied while I cared for our preemie in a little apartment next to my husband's work. One morning, when I realized I had changed *twelve* diapers by about 8am, I thought, "Look at me go." (And then I think I cried for a bit...)

You may never find yourself in a position where you're caring for three preschoolers at the same time (and I must say, I *really* love life now that everyone is potty-trained), but the point is that when you or the ones you love have to go through something alone, that can be a good thing.

3 - Sickness and pain can be a gift.

I want to explain this one because initially that can sound like crazy talk. Just hear me out...

The surgery I mentioned at the beginning of this chapter was one of a series of four that I received after suffering with health problems for more than a decade. Prior to that time, my mom and I didn't see each other very much. It wasn't that we didn't *want* to see each other, but the hour-long drive with so many little children going to and from her house typically left me exhausted and cranky by the time I got home. In addition to that, there were school drop-offs and pick-ups right in the middle of the day, and I desperately needed my naptime. My mom had some health issues of her own and didn't feel comfortable driving on the freeway very often, and so we stayed in touch by talking on the phone a couple of times a week.

However, when my health problems intensified, I needed to go to the doctor each week with my toddler in tow, and it felt impossible to do so by myself. Desperate for help and exhausted from the pain, my mom and I *made it work* for us to be together. I chose a doctor halfway between her house and mine, so she could easily meet me in the waiting room and watch two-year-old Spencer. (He thought she lived there...) She stayed overnight at our house sometimes—baking my daughter's 8th birthday cake, doing all the dishes, driving my children to school, and playing "Blue Moon" on the piano for all of us.

During that "year of surgeries," I saw her more than I had ever seen her since leaving for college. The very next year is when the Alzheimer's started. I know that wasn't a coincidence, and there is *no way* I'm going to let that lesson be lost on me.

I think of that often—when my children are up all night with the stomach flu, sleeping on the floor next to my bed, and calling out to me every 45 minutes—or when someone stays home from school for a "sick day." One of my children recently spent a full week in the hospital, which involved hours of time playing board games, walking the halls together, and choosing which foods to order from "room service." Pain and sickness, though never fun and never sought after, give us a reason to be together.

I don't know if there will ever come a day when I won't have the urge to call my mom and tell her I need her. However, as I consider this full life we've spent together, and as I contemplate all that I learned from her example, I can now see that it's my turn. Each of us has the opportunity to *really be there* for our family members, and I consider that to be an absolute privilege.

> ➤ **QUESTIONS:** When have you been there for someone who needed you? When has someone been there for you? How do you feel about your current availability to those who you love?

➤ **CHALLENGE:** Consider your best memories with your loved ones and the strength of your current relationships. Identify one way you can more fully "be there" for the ones who need you most.

CHAPTER 16

The Best 12 Minutes of the Day

What simple rituals shape our lives?

Have you ever heard about "the best nine minutes" of the day?

My friend Tricia taught me about them one afternoon while we were sitting on the beach, watching our families play in the sand and in the waves.

Tricia had been taking parenting classes in preparation for the adoption of her foster son, and the instructor had told her that there were nine minutes of the day that could have the greatest impact on our children:

- The first three minutes of the morning

- The three minutes after they get home from school

- The three minutes before they go to bed

I *love* that idea, and as I shared it online, I watched it resonate with thousands and thousands of parents everywhere—because it is so doable.

As I think back on my life, I realize that my mom was the *master* at this, creating precious rituals that fit this structure exactly. She, however, added three *additional* minutes to this formula that became particularly sweet for me.

I'll take you through our typical scenarios.

The First Three Minutes of the Morning:

We'd pad out to the front room, in our footy pajamas or fuzzy socks, and she would most likely be sitting on the couch, snuggled under a cozy lap blanket, and surrounded by spiritual reading materials. Her eyes would *light up* as she said, every morning, "Ahhh, look who woke up!" Ask any of her children how, *exactly*, she said that greeting, and you'll receive identical answers. It was with enthusiasm, with deep love, and with just a hint of surprise—as though she had not expected to see such a precious child come into the room that morning.

Not once did she give the impression that we were bothering her or interrupting her solitude. In fact, I don't think that ever crossed her mind. It was as though she were saying, "You are the focus of my life, and when you are here with me, nothing else matters."

The First Three Minutes After Getting Home:

Whether arriving home from school, an outing with Dad, or an activity with friends, *every single time* I walked through the door, my mom would call out, "You're home! At laaaaaast!" And when *she* would get home—from grocery shopping or other errands—we would say the same to her.

This phrase was said with the exact same love as the morning greeting, but the tone was just a little different. It was as though she were saying, "I have been thinking of you every minute, watching the clock and hoping that you would walk through that door. This house is not the same without you. I love you and miss you when you are away from me. What a beautiful privilege it is to have you home again."

Then, if I had been on an adventure—like a trip to a museum or a special school dance—or if I'd just taken a big test, she would invite me to sit down next to her on the couch or on her bed, and with the enthusiasm of a college roommate, she'd say, "Now tell me all about it from beginning to end!"

I would talk and talk and talk, and she would listen to every word.

The Three Minutes Before We Went to Bed:

Bedtimes weren't enforced in our home (I have *no idea* how my parents survived all those years, but my dad's a night owl, and he liked to have us with him), and so our "tuck in" routine was sporadic. Sometimes I would put myself to bed early, occasionally I would watch *The Late Show* with my dad, and sometimes I would work for hours on homework (with a gentle caution from my mom, "Don't stay up *too* late!"). Regardless of the *time* I went to bed, however, the goodnight phrases were the same (and they were always said with the highest enthusiasm):

She would blow kisses at me in rapid succession and then say these phrases:

Je t'aime! ("I love you" in French)

À demain! ("See you tomorrow" in French)

Hasta mañana! ("See you tomorrow" in Spanish)

This was entertaining, to say the least, because my mom had *such* a hard time learning new languages, but knowing a few phrases brought *absolute delight* to her voice. I usually went to sleep giggling—thinking about how *cute* she was.

The Three Extra Minutes I Mentioned?

They took place right before we would leave the house.

When we were younger—preparing to walk to our elementary school or getting in the car with Dad to go on an outing—she would run out to the porch and pretend like she was Cinderella saying goodbye to the fairy godmother as she was going off to the ball (Mom played the part of Cinderella). With one arm waving cheerfully and with an enormous smile on her face, she would call, "Goodbye-ee! Goodbye-ee!"

As we got older, if one of us were there at her house for a visit with our children, and if we were driving off to return to our own homes, she would pretend that she was going to chase the car (and she did for about 20 yards) while the grandchildren squealed, "Run, Grandma, run!"

After her knee surgeries, when running down the street wouldn't work anymore, she got this idea to do the Macarena while we drove away. That way, she could stand in place, but she could still get us to laugh and smile while we said goodbye.

In fact, about a year into Mom's Alzheimer's, I was at her home during a physical therapy appointment. Once the stretching and exercises were done, the nurse filled out her paperwork and prepared to leave. "Have you ever done the Macarena?" my mom asked, her voice full of curiosity.

"Well, no, I haven't," the nurse replied warily.

"Oh, you *must!*" my mom replied, as though it would be an absolute crime to send this poor woman out the door without learning the Macarena arm motions.

Even though my mom could barely walk, she stood up next to our picture window in the front room, insisted that the nurse stand directly in front of her, and then put *me* at the front of the line to teach the Macarena. We danced for about three minutes, and I could hardly stop laughing. It was so ridiculous and *so fun* at the same time. The nurse left our house with an amused smile that day.

When I was a senior in high school and had to leave the house before 6am for a morning class at church, I wasn't very good about waking up on my own. I had way too many extracurricular activities (in retrospect), and the alarm clock seemed to go off entirely too early. Mom knew this, and so just about every morning, she would make some hot chocolate for me and toast a bagel, and bring it into my room on a tray. "Good morning, April!" she would softly say as she placed the tray next to my bed. "Would you like to get up now?"

Then while I dressed, she would make my lunch, and if the weather was cold, she would warm up the car and defrost the windows so it would be ready for me to drive. (I am *not* this doting on my own children, and I have to remind myself that most of her children were out of the house at this point, and so she had the time and energy to do all this, but the point isn't how *much* she did for me. The point is how sweetly she *did* it.)

This idea of the best 9 (or 12) minutes means a lot to me, and I think about it daily. Sometimes our morning routine gets so busy that I focus too much on the *doing* and not enough on the fact that I have four beautiful children who woke up healthy and happy that day.

I *ache* for more quiet in my life (that's what recharges me), and so when I'm sending my children off to school, I sometimes might give the impression that I'm glad they're going...which is *so* sad. One time, while walking out of our home office, keys in hand, I accidentally said to my husband, "I'm going to get rid of the kids, and I'll be right back." Then realizing my error, I said, "I mean, I'm going to go *take the kids to school*, and I'll be right back." Eric wouldn't let me get out of that one.

Sometimes I'm finishing up computer work when my children walk through the door after school (because I always want to do more in one day than is humanly possible), and my boys, who get home first, have to compete with that "one last email" I'm trying to answer before we have our daily smoothie party.

Then at night, when I'm tired and *still* have things to do before I can rest, I'm not always patient and sweet when it's time to tuck everyone into bed.

Honestly, I cringe when I think of some of those "last three minutes" of the day.

But I have hope.

I think of my mom, and I think about all the things I *am* doing right, and I realize that this is all about progress.

Lately, when my "snugglers" (Grace or Spencer) come into my room early in the morning, I open my arms wide, just like my mom. When the children walk out the front door to go to school, I say, "Goodbye, precious children! I love you with all my heart and soul!" When they come home, I shut my computer, welcome them home, and make a smoothie—just about every single day. And at nighttime, I do my very best to add in a few more back tickles and hugs. It's not totally consistent, but I'm trying.

Some of it must be sinking in, though, because the other afternoon, as I was leaving the house to run errands, my son Ethan came out on the front porch and started doing the Macarena. Best moment of my day.

> *QUESTION:* What are some of the "best 12 minute" rituals in your family?

> *CHALLENGE:* What could you do to make those few minutes each day just a little more special?

Lessons on Faith

CHAPTER 17

Everybody Else's Mom is Better Dressed

Where do you get your confidence?

"Mom, do you ever feel intimidated around all the other moms?"

I was nine years old, and my mother had just returned from a PTA meeting at our local elementary school. I knew how the other moms looked. They had beautiful earrings and designer clothes. Their hair looked "just right," and some of them spent time at the tanning salon. From my perspective, the other mothers had an air of sophistication, but *my* mother was, well, not like that.

Mom's hair was going gray, and though she had nice outfits to wear on date night, her everyday clothes were typically purchased on sale...*not* from a department store. She put on make-up and brushed her hair nicely, and her kindness made up for whatever she might have been "lacking" physically. However, since I always felt insecure around my beautiful friends, I assumed the same held true for her.

I was wrong.

"No, April, I don't feel intimidated," she said gently. "Do you want to know why?"

I nodded.

"Because I look around the room, and I think, "No one here loves the Lord *more* than I do. They might love Him *as much* as I do, but they can't possibly love Him more because I love Him with all my heart."

I have never forgotten those words. They come back to me often. And whether your understanding of the Divine is the same as mine or not, I think we can agree that there is power when we know our worth isn't measured by what everyone else can see.

I'd like to share a few principles where, regardless of our religious or spiritual beliefs, we can find common ground around this subject. My examples will reflect my own experience, but I'm hopeful you can easily adapt these ideas to your own life.

Here's one common-ground principle: Whatever it is that grounds us—that helps us to know our true value—it needs to be deep in our hearts.

I remember at least one such experience.

One evening, as a high school student, I was talking with my mother in the kitchen about cars, houses, careers, and other goals for the future. It was a casual conversation (nothing earth-shattering), but then my mom got quiet and said, "One thing that helps my perspective is to remember that the 'things' in our lives pale in comparison to the *Real Power*. You see, there is no possession in the world—not the biggest house, not the fastest car, not the most extravagant outfit—that can bring tears to my eyes just by thinking about it."

I looked directly into her eyes at that point, and there was a long pause while she gave me a glimpse into her heart. For those moments, she let me feel how much she loved the Lord. I remember the power of that experience—as both of us were visibly touched by the sweetness of the moment—and I promised myself that I would do all I could to live with and develop that same conviction.

There was nothing "surface" about that experience. The power penetrated deeply.

Another common-ground principle is that we need to make time to connect with that core strength on a regular basis.

I saw this modeled by the frequency in which I found my mom on her knees. Honestly, I've lost count of how many times I walked into her room and found her kneeling in prayer, her head resting on her clasped hands, and her mind clearly pouring out her heart to God. There's a peace that fills you when you know your parents speak with the Divine—and this wasn't just done in public places like church or in the dining room before a family dinner. These were quiet moments when no one else could see, and when the prayers could be long and sweet.

What I especially loved, however, was what she did when I barged in mid-prayer.

You would think she would have done one of two things: kept praying (so I would have realized I had interrupted and slowly backed out of the room) or gently whispered, "I'm having a prayer, but I'll be out soon."

No, she did something completely different. Every single time she heard the door open while she was praying, she *immediately* turned toward the door with her arms open wide and a huge, welcoming smile on her face—almost as though she were saying, "Here you are! I was hoping you would come see me."

One day, I felt especially curious, and I asked, "Mom, what do you say to God when I interrupt your prayer?"

She smiled, and, with a little twinkle in her eye, said, "I just tell Him my child needs me, and I'll be right back."

As I'm sure you can guess, seeing my mother regularly connect with that precious power she received from above greatly impacted *my* personal habits. As I've raised my own children, they've often walked in on me praying—kneeling atop my tall bed and asking the Lord for help before I start my day. I always open my arms—just like she did—and it's sweet to see that exchange from the other side. But by far the sweetest experience I've had yet was when I recently walked quietly into my daughter's room and saw *her* kneeling in prayer.

How each person defines and connects with the Divine is unique, but as this connection regularly *happens*, there is a beautiful power.

A final common-ground principle is that we need to remember to *access* that power in our daily lives because it is available to us at all times, even in the small but hard moments of the day.

My mother, it seems, *never* forgot to ask for that power. In fact, I used to laugh at how *often* she asked for it...like that Saturday morning she gathered us in prayer before we went garage sale-ing to ask for help finding *just* the right play pen and high chair for my older sister, who was looking for gently-used baby gear on a budget. (We found it.)

Looking back, it seems silly that I ever even *tried* to compare my mom to other women at the PTA meetings who seemed more fashionable than she was. And when we feel discouraged about the areas where *we* are lacking, we need to remember that confidence doesn't come from our physique or our home decor or our clothes.

It comes when we acknowledge that there is a power out there greater than our own. It comes when we let that power go deep into our hearts. And it comes when we remember to turn to that power frequently—especially when life feels impossible. Because even though it might feel that way sometimes, my mother showed me that we can absolutely do this.

> ➢ **QUESTION:** How closely are *you* connected with that power that is greater than your own? How close would you like to be?

> ➢ **CHALLENGE:** Find a few minutes today...and every day...to connect more deeply or more regularly, and then record what changes you see in your life.

CHAPTER 18

No, You Are Not Ugly

Whose opinion matters?

One of my defining moments happened during a lunch break when I was in elementary school.

We lived just a block away from the school, and I skipped home practically every day to eat a cup of Campbell's vegetable soup and a slice of whole-wheat toast with my mom. She would stop the sweeping, move the bills off to the side of the table, and sit with me for the 20 or 30 minutes I was home . . . simply letting me tell her all about my morning and what our class's plans were for the afternoon.

But one day, I came home in tears.

My mom immediately opened her arms to me and said, "Oh, April, what's the matter?" Then she led me out to the living room and sat down beside me on our soft brown couch, holding my hands and looking into my eyes--trying to figure out what on earth could be troubling me so much.

I poured out my heart and, through my sobs, told her how a girl at school had told another girl (who then relayed the message back to me) that she thought I was ugly.

Looking back, I can see that this was just one of those things girls do--growing up and figuring yourself out is a challenge. This particular classmate and I later became good friends, but at the time, I was *devastated*.

My mom then told me two things.

First, she said, "April, you are not ugly."

I appreciated hearing that from her, but it didn't really help. She was my *mom*. Of course she was going to say that.

But the second thing she told me has stayed with me for the last 20+ years, and I count it as a moment that helped shape the rest of my life.

"You must remember that the only thing that matters is what the *Lord* thinks of you. Is the Lord pleased with you, April?"

I thought for a moment--about how I tried so hard to be a good girl, how I tried to love other people and work hard in school and obey my parents and help people who felt sad. I thought about how I felt when I prayed and when I read holy words. I knew I wasn't perfect, but I knew that I was living a life that would please God.

I looked up at my mom and nodded my head.

Seeing the sincerity in my expression, she replied, "Then *nothing else matters.*"

That phrase sat in my heart, and I knew it was true.

At the end of that lunch break, I walked back to school with the most peaceful feeling inside.

I hadn't gotten any prettier while I was home, but as I crossed the street and entered the gate to the playground, it simply didn't matter anymore.

Even though I'm no longer an adolescent, there are still moments I start to worry about what others think of me. My work online is very public. I pour out my heart on a regular basis. I show people pictures of the messes on my counters. I let everyone see my wrinkles and the dark circles under my eyes.

However, these words from my mom come back to me often, and every time I think of them, I feel that same peaceful feeling.

We all have times when we wonder if we are enough. And there will never be a shortage of exchanges--deliberate or accidental--that hurt our feelings.

But we can strengthen our resolve and remind ourselves that ultimately there are very few opinions that carry weight. Our job is to identify whose opinions those are...and then *remember* them.

> *QUESTION:* Whose opinions *really* matter in your life? Have you had any specific experiences that helped you learn (or teach) this lesson?

> *CHALLENGE:* Take a moment to record the names of three or four individuals whose opinions you absolutely trust. (I included God in my list...) The next time you feel down about yourself, think about these people and remind yourself what *they* would say to you.

CHAPTER **19**

You've Got to Touch the Post!

How do we get help from above?

Prior to her Alzheimer's, my mom *loved* taking her morning walk on a wooden-planked pathway along the beach just minutes from our house. She sang as she walked, admired the sweeping views of the Long Beach harbor, and sometimes took one or two of us with her—if we weren't sleeping in or otherwise occupied with another activity.

At the end of the path, there's a short wall with a little wooden post in the middle, and before we *ever* turned around to walk back to our car, my mom would say, "You have to touch!"

So we always did...like in a relay race where you tag the end point and hurry back to the start.

One day, however, I noticed that my mom wasn't just tagging the post quickly and heading back down the boardwalk, like I was. She touched it gently, closed her eyes with a soft smile, and *then* went on her way.

I asked her what she was doing, and she said, "Every time I touch this post, I say quietly in my mind, 'I consecrate my day to the Lord.' Then I think about Him through the whole day and try to please Him in everything I do."

I couldn't help but be touched by her faith and sweetness, so *of course* I adopted the same ritual. Sometimes when we would reach the post at the exact same time, we would smile at each other and say aloud, "We consecrate our day to the Lord!" Then we would hold hands and walk the rest of the way back—feeling a little more excited about the day ahead.

To this day, whenever our family goes on a walk or takes a hike that goes up and back the exact same path, we find some end point--a stop sign, a fence, or a tree—and do exactly as we've been taught.

It adds a special element to the experience, and it inspires us to remember that each day of our lives is a joint effort between a Higher Power and us. We do all we can, and then we ask for help to make up the rest.

The reason why I love that story so much is because it reminds me that it is totally possible to get daily help from above.

Whether or not you like to go for daily walks, you can attach a small, spiritual ritual into your daily routine to remind you of the help that is available from your Higher Power. Perhaps it could be something you do each day when you walk to the mailbox. Maybe you could add a simple image or quote to your screen saver or digital wallpaper. It's so helpful to have something in place that inspires us to remember what we know is true.

I don't know if you're like me, but I tend to slip into "worrying mode" on a regular basis. For example, three letters from our insurance company are sitting in my inbox right now...each one requiring a substantial amount of time and effort to reach a resolution. I've also got a pivotal decision weighing on my mind that I have *no idea* how to make. And in the background are those little questions that keep tugging on my subconscious:

> *Am I spending enough time with each child? Is it possible for me to be more nurturing to my neighbor who is struggling? Should I make it a priority to finally decorate all those blank walls downstairs?*

Yes, some of our responsibilities are fairly trivial, but others matter more than we realize. How do we access help from that Source who intimately knows what we need?

One of the most poignant answers I received to this question came when I simply observed what my mom did when she thought she was alone.

It was common for her to sing while she cleaned the kitchen, chopped vegetables, or prepared dinner. I would position myself at the dining room table or on a couch in the living room while I completed my homework—the happy noises from the kitchen a comforting background.

On more than one occasion, her singing would stop, and I would hear her whisper—as though she were calling for help, "Father." Then it would be quiet, while she listened for the response.

I asked her about that one day—why she always called for Father.

"Sometimes I'm struggling with something that I don't know how to solve. And so it's like a little prayer. I am asking Him for strength. I'm asking Him to help me know what to do."

Until I became an adult, and especially until I had a family of my own, I didn't quite understand the kinds of burdens that she was carrying.

Now I have a pretty good idea.

Everyone has hard things going on in their lives. Once, when speaking to a room of about 200 people, I asked each person to write down the main challenge on his or her mind. After about 30 seconds, I said, "Now raise your hand if you couldn't think of anything." Everyone laughed.

Of *course* you're struggling. I am too. But honestly, when we focus our faith, when we consecrate each day to the One who gives us life, and when we remember *in the moment* to ask for sustaining help, it most definitely comes.

> ➤ *QUESTION:* What is a daily ritual that *you* could adopt to help you more fully connect with a Higher Power?

> ➤ **CHALLENGE:** At some point today, take a moment to write down the heaviest thoughts on your mind—and then ask specifically for help from above.

CHAPTER 20

The Hole in the Nylons

Will miracles happen for you?

If there's one thing that all of us would like to see *more* of in our lives, it's miracles. Wouldn't you agree? I *yearn* for miracles. I pray for them. I hope for them. And one of the reasons I know they are possible is because I've seen them happen over and over again in the life of my mother.

This is one of my favorite stories, simple as it may be, that reminds me to trust that miracles can happen.

One Sunday morning, many years ago, as my mother was getting ready for church, she realized that she had a hole in her nylons, several inches above her shoe line. She searched *everywhere* in her dresser for another pair, but to no avail. Reaching down to her ankles, she tried to stretch the nylons every which way—hoping that perhaps she could hide the hole inside her shoe or under her skirt, but no matter how much she tried, that hole sat in the same spot.

For a proper woman like my mother, having this gaping hole was somewhat of a catastrophe, but it was time to go to church, and she couldn't spend any more time worrying about those nylons.

Taking just a moment to herself before joining the rest of the family, she gently offered a prayer: "Father, I'm so sorry that I didn't check my nylons yesterday, and I'm sorry I don't have an extra pair. I want to look my very best as I go to worship Thee, but for today, this will have to do."

She then helped get all of her children into the car, drove to church (my dad, who had early morning meetings, was already there), and sat down with the family on our regular pew.

A few minutes later, still feeling badly about her nylons, she glanced down at her leg.

The hole was *gone.*

She felt around the sides of her calf, up by her knees, and down by her ankles, but she couldn't find the hole *anywhere.*

Completely puzzled by this point, she took off her shoe, and there—on the *very* bottom of her foot—was the hole.

I heard this story dozens of times while I was growing up. "April," she told me, "There was *no way* that hole could have moved to the bottom of my foot. I had done everything I could to try to position it there. The Lord helped me that day. He understood what I needed, and that was a little blessing He sent just for me."

Now I know that this seems like such a simple, inconsequential thing, but the lesson it basically shouts is that *miracles happen.* And they'll happen for *you.*

I remember one Saturday afternoon, when I needed to get five-year-old Grace to her last soccer game of the season. My husband had planned to go with me to help with our two-month-old baby and our other two children, but a last-minute urgent need from a neighbor required his assistance, and I told him I would be fine.

Once we arrived at the soccer field, I heard Grace gasp, "I forgot my socks and my soccer cleats!"

We were all devastated. There was no time to return home, this was her very last game, and there was no way they would let her play without shoes and socks.

Having learned from my mother's example (over and over again), I gathered my children around me in the parking lot, and we offered a prayer—apologizing for forgetting the socks and cleats and asking that, if it were possible, Grace would be able to play her game.

We approached the field in faith, and moments later, we ran into a friend of ours whose son had just finished his game. As we explained our plight, our friend said, "Why doesn't she wear Braden's socks and cleats? He's the same size as Grace!" We thought that was an excellent idea, so our two five-year-olds sat on the grass and made the transfer. It was perfect.

These kinds of miracles happen often. They're always timed "just right," and they remind me in such a powerful way that *we are not alone.*

One of my very favorite miracles happened on my birthday a couple of years ago—shortly after my mom was diagnosed with Alzheimer's—when she was in a rehabilitation center for a broken hip.

As a special treat, my husband stayed home with our four children and sent me to visit her alone for the day. During the one-hour drive, I was thinking about a list of questions I had written down that morning— things I was hoping the Lord would help me to understand about my life's course, like how I felt I was continually stretched too thin and that my efforts simply didn't measure up.

Though I felt sweetness during the drive and an immense feeling of support, I didn't receive any specific answers to my questions.

When I arrived at the center, I was privileged to have a wonderful lunch with my dad, my sister Laura, and a neighbor of ours who had come to visit. I sat next to my mom and held her hand as much as I could. She was quiet, but happy. This was a blessing by itself because, up to that point, she hadn't been doing very well. She had been crying a lot and repeatedly asking when she could go home.

The nurses had explained that she kept trying to find a way out. One day they found her *way* out in the corner of the facility by the vending machines. Other days, she would sit by the emergency exit. One time she made the alarm go off.

But that day, she was calm and happy—totally at ease.

Now there are two very special things about the visit that I feel I can share.

The first is that they served birthday cake that day.

Once a month, the facility celebrates all of the residents' birthdays at the same time.

I asked the nurses if they always serve cake on the 19th, and they said no, that it changes every month.

Then it struck me that this was a tender mercy from the Lord. On my birthday, when I got to go spend the day with my mom—who I missed so much—He arranged for them to have cake.

The second special part of the day was a sweet experience I had while my mom and I were sitting alone in the lobby together. I had my arms wrapped around her, and she started speaking very quietly--almost indistinctly.

I listened closer, and I could hear that she was giving me counsel and advice.

Moving my ear as close to her lips as I could, I soon realized that in her calm, encouraging, beautiful voice, she was answering the *exact* questions I had written down for the Lord that morning.

I won't record the specifics because it was such a sacred moment, and the counsel was just for me, but this was one of the most precious miracles I have ever received in my entire life.

My mom has had dementia (which developed into Alzheimer's) for pretty much the entire time I have been running my websites. She doesn't know how to use the Internet, and she isn't involved in my day-to-day life. But as we sat together, and as she talked to me about my responsibilities, my choices, my struggles, my heart, my goals, and my daily work with my family and with my organizations, it was as though she knew *everything*. I can't even think about the experience without getting choked up. *No one* besides the Lord could have known what to say to me, and He chose to deliver that message through the voice of the one from whom I needed to hear it the most.

I hesitated to even write anything about this experience—because some things are just so special that you don't want to put them out in front of the world. But in this case, I feel like He wants me to share this so that if you are struggling, you will know that He is aware of you, too.

I have zero doubt in the Lord's capacity to perform miracles. I know He loves all of His children--from every religion and background. He knows we all make mistakes and that we struggle and that we need help. And when we turn to Him, He has a limitless ability to supply everything we need.

Miracles happen. They are beautiful. And they are available for *all* of us.

➤ *QUESTION:* What miracles have you seen in your life—or in the lives of those you love?

➤ *CHALLENGE:* Watch closely to see the hand of God in your life, and then record those blessings and miracles so you can share them with those who will benefit from your faith.

CHAPTER 21

To Those with Brave Faces

What comforting words do you need to hear?

I've noticed something that happens often to the people I love: They suffer something deep, and very personal. So personal, in fact, that they can't discuss it with anyone but *maybe* a few of their closest friends. Sometimes—even if they *can* discuss it—the challenge lasts so long and involves so many painful emotions that bringing it up over and over again isn't socially acceptable.

So they chalk it up as "one of those things I have to get through" or they tell themselves, "this is just life," and then they put on brave faces while they endure the difficult days—and sometimes sleepless middle-of-the-nights—alone.

Let me give you some examples.

I have a friend who has been fearlessly starting a new business—not because she wants to, but because her husband's health took a major turn for the worse, and she is now the full-time provider and caregiver for her family.

Another friend is in the middle of a seemingly-endless string of court dates—trying to get custody of her child from an emotionally abusive spouse.

Others are struggling with financial ruin, mental illness, betrayal, and addictions that put an incredible strain on their family relationships.

One friend of mine, whose child with special needs was slowly coming to the close of her life, posted that she walked through the store one day—wearing sweats, not having showered for days, because she was sitting by the bedside of her dying daughter. She noted that everyone seemed so normal around her—just going about their days, buying dish detergent and paper towels, and she felt like calling out, "Do you see me? Do you know what I am going through? I am not okay!!!!"

There are dozens more examples I could give here, but I think you get the point. More often than not, the people around us—those who we love, and those who we don't love *yet*—are wearing brave faces. It's likely that *you're* doing the same in at least one aspect of your life right now.

And the whole reason I'm bringing this up is because I want you to know what my mom would have said to you if you came over to our house and sat by her on the couch and poured out your heart. This was her *specialty.*

First she would have listened. She would have asked you to tell her all about it. She would have let you share every detail—without ever looking bored or nonverbally suggesting you "get to the point." I know this because that's what she did for me and my siblings—and her friends who would drop by—and her friends who would call her on the phone. I remember resting next to her on her bed for what seemed like hours while she held the phone to her ear simply saying—at just the right times, in a totally compassionate voice, "Oh, I see," or "I'm sorry," or "Yes, that must have been awful."

When I was younger, I would whisper, "Will you please get off the phone?" and she would hold up one finger to her lips, as if to say, "Shhh." But as I got older, I would just snuggle up to her so she would put her arm around me and wait patiently until the call finished. It was like watching a surgeon perform a life-saving operation. Each call was Mom healing a heart.

After listening to your story, she would have told you exactly what you needed to hear—which would obviously vary according to your specific challenge—but if someone had hurt you, she would have said, "They had no right to do that to you. I'm so sorry for them that they think they need to treat other people that way. You deserve better than that." Then she would *always* say, "You need to keep doing what you know is right, and if that person who hurt you wants to continue acting that way, that's *their* SDB." (Self-defeating behaviors...she read a book about those once and then made sure we all understood what they were.)

If you were going through a sickness or physical pain, she would say, "That is so difficult. I am sorry you are in so much pain. You know, God *has* to give you challenges so that you can grow. And since you're such a strong person, and He knows you can handle *so* much, He gave you this. He had to think of *something* that would be hard for you!" Then she would add, with all sincerity, "If it were possible, I would ask God to give that pain to *me* so I could carry it for you." Honestly, I know she would have followed through. I still hear her voice saying, "I wish it were me going through that, April."

If you simply made a mistake—did something foolish that you totally regretted—she would have put her arm around you and said, "There, there. Think of all the good things that you do. You don't need to worry about this anymore. You can make things right again, and think of all that you've learned now."

And if you were scared—because the challenge required you to step up and do something totally outside your comfort zone—she would have said, "If anyone in the *world* can do this, it's you. This is what you were *made* for. This is who you *are*. People need you, and you are going to get through this with flying colors!"

Then she'd usually add something like, "I'm *proud* of you. I know this isn't easy, but look—you're *doing* it!"

Essentially, she'd make you feel like a million bucks.

Then, as the conversation was coming to a close, she would remind you where you could turn for help once you left her presence.

"You *must* remember that you are not going through this alone. The Lord is with you every single day. He knows *exactly* what you are going through, and if you ever need *any* help, He will give that to you. There's no need to be afraid. There's no need to worry. You are being protected and lifted. Angels will be on your right hand and on your left. And you will feel that power. You will know that what I am saying is true."

As I'm writing this, my mind is flashing back to countless phone calls from my college dorm room and countless mother-daughter counseling sessions at the kitchen table or while sitting on her bed or while eating frozen yogurt in a warm car. It was such a natural process of my life:

I go through something hard ——> I call my mom ——> She tells me exactly what I need to hear ——> I increase my faith in God ——> I feel better ——> I grow ——>I get stronger. (Rinse and repeat.)

While it's hard to record these memories, I don't think I can cover this topic without addressing the brave face my *mother* wore as her Alzheimer's was settling in. She knew something wasn't right. She heard my dad whispering his concerns to me one afternoon, and, once he left the room, she said, in a frustrated voice, "What was he telling you? Did he say I'm losing my memory? Because I am just fine. I may be missing some details, but I haven't *totally* lost my marbles."

Those months and years were the hardest. We all knew something wasn't right, but we didn't know how to help her. One afternoon, my sister Laura sat with Mom in the car parked in front of the house and started the conversation, "Mom, we think that you are losing your memory."

They talked for a long time, and, at one point, Mom said, "Do you *really* think so, Laura? Do you really think my memory is going?"

Laura replied as gently as she could, "Mom, we've actually had this same conversation before."

I can't even imagine what was happening inside my mother's head as she realized what was taking place. That transition time was heartbreaking because life, as she knew it, was falling apart. For example, she couldn't remember when she had last showered or washed her clothes, and if one of us offered to help her into the shower, she would completely shut down—like a toddler having a battle of wills with a parent.

One day, she called our friend three times to RSVP to a baby shower: "Hello, Sarah! Thank you so much for the invitation to the shower. I would love to attend, and I would like to contribute to the group gift!"

"Did she ever make it or contribute to the group gift?" I asked Sarah in a later conversation.

"Oh no!" Sarah responded with a compassionate smile, "But I know she had every intention of doing so. I mean, she called *three times*, bless her heart."

I remember another night when she got upset with my dad because he wouldn't let her go teach a shorthand class that ended more than 40 years ago. My daughter Alia and I couldn't calm her, so I sat by Mom while Alia made a phone call from the other room. In her best "school administrator" voice, Alia reassured her that the class had actually been canceled that night, but the school appreciated her work as a teacher, and they would be sure to call her if another opportunity came up. That finally settled her.

Because Mom isn't able to comprehend what's happening anymore, I feel like the "brave face" has shifted to us: her children and her husband. We miss her more than we can explain. I can still hug her and kiss her and talk with her, but when she tries to respond, she can't remember how to put more than a few words together.

I feel somewhat selfish thinking of my own pain right now, when she can't even get out of her bed or care for her own basic needs, but when you have a mortal angel by your side for your entire life, and then that angel is silenced, you have to learn how to fill that hole.

Fortunately, I have five sisters. They know Mom, and they know what she would have said, so sometimes I call them and say, "I'm sorry to bother you, but I would have called Mom right now, and I just need someone to tell me everything will be okay." And my sisters get it. We talk, and they let me cry, and we laugh about funny things Mom would have said, and there's a comfort there I can't describe.

One time recently, when my life felt so heavy that it hurt to breathe, I had a few moments alone with Mom—sitting on the edge of her hospital bed, holding her hands and looking into her eyes.

"I'm hurting, Mom." I told her.

"You are?" she asked, with concerned eyes—just like before.

"Yes," I responded. "And I know you can't talk to me, but maybe I could just tell you what's happening, and I can say what I think you would say?"

She nodded—never breaking eye contact.

So I thought back to all of our previous conversations, and I repeated the kinds of things I had heard her say to me and many others, and as I spoke, she kept nodding and looking at me with her signature compassion, as though she *totally* understood (because I think she did).

And at that point I realized that it's okay that she can't speak anymore. She's taught me well. She's said it all before. And while I'm writing all this down so my *own* children and I will be able to read it, I'm also writing it down so her beauty and wisdom can help *you*.

Wearing a brave face isn't easy. It's necessary, and it's a sign of maturity, and there's undoubtedly a ton of growth going on behind it, but because you are probably wearing that face more often than not, I thought it would be helpful to let you know that you are not alone. You're going to get through this. And I, for one, am very, very proud of you.

> ➤ *QUESTION:* Are you currently wearing a brave face? What are the comforting words you need to hear?

➢ *CHALLENGE:* Take a moment to record the best advice you've received—or perhaps record one of the ideas in this chapter that resonated with you. Keep this in a place where you can refer to it as needed.

More Lessons I'm Learning

CHAPTER 22

Even When She Doesn't Know Me

Does a mother's love ever end?

When our family learned that Mom had Alzheimer's, we started planning our "last" adventures. Knowing there would come a point when she would no longer be able to get out of bed or speak or smile, we decided it was worth the extra effort to create special memories together.

One of these adventures consisted of a trip to Disneyland with a grandson who was sponsored by the Make-a-Wish Foundation. Several members of the family joined together at the park, and we spent the day going on rides, enjoying the shows, treasuring our time together, and taking all kinds of photos for our memory books.

One of the sweetest experiences of the day happened right before we left the park.

My sister Lisa and I had taken Mom to the restroom, and on the way back to our group, Mom was acting quite confused. It had been a long day, and she was exhausted.

"I am not your mother," she told Lisa. "I am the person who is your mother when your real mother can't be here."

"Who am I?" Lisa asked softly.

"You know who you are," Mom responded—trying to brush off the question.

"Yes, *I* know who I am, but do *you* know who I am?"

Mom paused for a moment. She brought Lisa around right in front of her, and Lisa knelt down so she was looking directly into Mom's eyes.

They sat there for a few seconds—Lisa with a sweet smile, hoping Mom would know her name (but realizing she probably didn't), and Mom searching Lisa's face deeply, waiting for *something* to trigger her memory.

Finally she gave the best answer she could give, and her words have been playing over and over again in my mind ever since.

She simply said, "I know I love you . . . *very* much."

Lisa nodded. "Yes, you do. And I love you too."

After that tender conversation, I didn't know what to say. Kneeling down by Mom's side, I started showing her all the photos from our time together that I had on my camera. I pointed to each person and told her all of our names. I didn't even *want* to ask her if she knew my name at that point because (a) it's got to be extremely frustrating for her, and (b) I wasn't ready for that to happen yet—to have my mother look me directly in the eyes and not know who I was.

Instead, I decided to tell myself what I know is true—that even if she doesn't know my name, and even if she forgets that she's my mom, she loves me (and *all* her children) very much.

Over the past few years, I've developed a special love for those flowers called "forget-me-nots."

In fact, "Forget Me Not" could very well be my personal theme. It's that phrase that keeps running through my head every time my children and I make our Thursday drive to Long Beach to take care of my mom. It's that phrase I think about whenever we get to her house and I'm about to look her in the eyes for the first time in a week. It's that phrase I've been living with ever since the very first moment I sensed that something wasn't right.

Please, Mom...please don't forget me.

I held onto that fear for *years*—the fear that the day would come when my mother would look me straight in the eye and have no recollection of any of the moments we had experienced together.

Well, I remember clearly when that day finally came.

It was during one of my regular weekly visits, and she simply didn't know me...at all.

Sometimes I was her granddaughter, and sometimes I was one of my sisters. At one point, I was a student in the shorthand class she taught for a few years at our local college.

I guess it really shouldn't have mattered because she still hugged me, kissed me, sang with me, and even wiped a little tear that had escaped down my cheek, but as I drove home that night with sleeping children in the van, I simply couldn't hold myself together.

Since that night, Mom surprised me by saying my name a few times. One evening, while we were chopping vegetables together, I said casually and cheerfully, "I love you, Mom." She replied softly, "I love you, too, April."

I had to turn my head so my change in emotion wouldn't surprise her. That response was more than I expected, and my name never sounded so sweet.

Now, at the time of this writing, she hasn't said my name in months— but I want to share an experience that happened with my daughters during last Thursday's visit.

While I was getting the dinner ingredients out of the trunk of our minivan, Alia and Grace ran into the house to see Grandma. She was in her wheelchair by the window, and after their helloes, the girls said, "Our mom is coming in soon. When you see her, say, 'Hi April!'"

They practiced with her over and over, and then when I walked in, Mom gave me a big smile and, with the girls by her side, slightly holding their breaths, she said, "Hi!"

My girls were so darling. They comforted me with, "We're sorry, Mom. We tried so hard to help her say your name."

I told them it was okay, and I let them know I appreciated their effort.

Later that night, however, while I was alone in my room, it struck me just *how* sweet that was of them. They're perceptive enough to know how much I would love to hear my mother say my name. They cherish our relationship and the time *we* have together. That fills me. That is a gift.

Every time I visit my mother, I still hope she'll recognize me. I picture her eyes lighting up, and I long for the familiar way she always said, "AY-pril!" But the pain has honestly faded over the years. She sees me as love. Her heart will never forget me, and my heart will certainly never forget her.

When you are about to lose someone, you come to understand what your relationship really means. And whether it's Alzheimer's, an illness, an accident, or a peaceful death that separates you, the pure love that binds a deliberate family will never ever end.

> ➤ *QUESTION:* If you could make one change in your life that would lead you closer to your ideal family relationship, what would that be?

> ➤ *CHALLENGE:* Do one thing this week to connect on a deeper level with one of your family members. Whether it's creating a special memory together, writing a letter of appreciation, or performing an act of service, identify one way you can intentionally strengthen your family.

CHAPTER 23

Don't Believe for One Minute that You're Failing

Whose voice helps us to see our lives clearly?

It was a year or two before my mom's memory started to go, and I visited her at the hospital for a couple of hours while she was recovering from a knee replacement surgery. She asked me how I was doing (that was just like my mom...asking *me* how I was while *she* was in the hospital bed).

I opened my heart to her and said, "Mom, I'm trying so hard, but I feel like I'm failing so often. Like today...I had these great intentions of teaching my girls piano lessons and playing with the children after school, but then I felt so tired that I just collapsed on the couch and cat-napped while they played with the train set and took turns on the computer."

My mom looked me in the eye and said, "April, you don't really believe you're failing, do you?"

I thought for a moment and then replied, "Well, yes, sometimes I do."

And then she said those words that I was aching to hear: "You must not listen to that negative voice for one minute. If you sit still, you'll hear another voice—a more powerful voice—telling you that you are doing a wonderful job."

She continued her encouragement for a couple more minutes, speaking simply and powerfully—right to my soul, and I said, "Mom, I need a tape recording of you telling me that."

To which she replied, "No, you don't need a tape recorder. You *know* this. It's in your heart. It's inside you from everything you have been taught. It's everything that you are."

I felt flooded with relief as I walked out to the hospital parking lot that evening. She was right. In spite of all the voices that are out there telling us that we're not doing enough or being enough, there is a quiet, more powerful, more accurate voice that helps us to see our lives clearly.

Now let's rewind to about 15 years before that day in the hospital.

It was my junior year of high school, and my mom carried around a heavily highlighted book called, *You Can't Afford the Luxury of a Negative Thought*. I have since read most of that book as a way to better understand what words inspired her and why she loved it so much. It is full of encouragement and facts explaining that our thoughts are linked so closely with our success in life that controlling them is *not* optional.

You might wonder why she needed a book like that, and here is where I want to carefully share why I think that was the case. The reason I use the word "carefully" is because I want to be loyal to my mother and keep personal things personal, but at the same time, I've found that discussing our humanness is essential when it comes to understanding one another.

The *main* struggle my mother had was with her weight and physical appearance.

My earliest memories of her include calorie-counting books and "sealing off" at 6pm so she wouldn't get into trouble and eat ice cream out of the freezer late at night. I didn't think much of those things—because it seemed like *most* of the adults in my life were also trying to lose weight by similar methods, but there is one moment seared into my memory that still stings when I think about it.

It was a late afternoon, and mom and I were getting ready to run an errand together. She popped into the restroom to comb her hair and apply a bit of lipstick, and I leaned against the doorframe to watch. I remember thinking how much I liked her curly black hair and her bright eyes. I thought her Clinique lipstick was the perfect shade. I loved her genuine smile and soft, huggable body. She embodied everything good and beautiful about life, and I wanted to be just like her.

After finishing her preparations, however, she assessed her reflection in the mirror, frowned a bit, and—possibly not realizing I was there—whispered to herself, "Terrible, terrible."

I remember catching my breath and wishing I had the words to help her see who she really was. I knew, by the way she treated others, that she saw everyone *else* as a beautiful work in progress, but for some reason, she simply couldn't see it in herself.

Around that same time, my sister Laura remembers going to a class on self-esteem with our mom. The first question the instructor asked them was to rate their self esteem on a scale of 1-10, with 1 being the lowest on the piece of paper they were given. Laura said, "I peeked over to see what Mom wrote, and my heart sank when I saw that she wrote '1.' I too did not know what to say or do to lift her up. She was perfect in every way to me."

So how did my mother overcome her feelings of failure and inadequacy? I think the best way to explain her growth process is with a few stories.

(As a quick side note, I don't think she ever stopped worrying about her weight, but I will say that's one of the benefits of Alzheimer's. She smiles and hugs us and lets us take pictures whenever we want, and she has no idea that anyone even *should* be concerned about appearances. I love that.)

One afternoon when I was in third grade, my mom and I were standing outside on the curb in front of our house. We'd just said goodbye to a friend who'd come to visit, and this friend looked like she'd just stepped out of a magazine. Her hair, make-up, clothing, and nails were perfect, and after she drove away, my mom looked down at her own nails, which were very weak, short, and unpolished, and she said, "My nails look awful, but I think it's time for me to go get some acrylics. I think it will give me a lift every time I look at my hands."

So she did. I don't think she'd ever paid for a manicure before in her life, but she found a little salon close to my high school and met some darling friends who kept her nails looking beautiful for years. Although she could never lose "those last 20 pounds," she put time and energy into doing what she *could*.

Additionally, mom worked hard every day on the things that mattered to her, but she didn't stress about perfection or demand optimal results. Instead, she focused totally on the process and evaluated herself on how hard she was trying.

For example, early in her 70s, she decided she wanted to learn Spanish. After living in Mexico on a church mission with my dad for 18 months—and not picking up the language as well as she'd hoped—she decided to enroll in a class at our local city college.

One day in class, my mom was feeling *totally* confused by all the new information and asked the instructor a series of questions, hoping for a little bit of compassion and extra help. I don't know who the instructor was, and clearly she didn't know she had an *angel* in her class, but she responded so unkindly to my mother (essentially saying, "You are not smart enough to be in here!") that my mother left the class with tears in her eyes and felt absolutely defeated.

She told me later how she sat on the city college lawn and asked God what she should do, as she felt so badly about her academic performance. The words that came to her mind, in reference to the teacher, were kind and calm: "You don't need her."

From that day—until the Alzheimer's began—my mother happily practiced Spanish on her own, carrying a small tape player with her and listening to recorded lessons whenever she wanted to do so.

Did she ever learn Spanish? Not really. But she was the cutest thing in the world—practicing with energy and enthusiasm and throwing out occasional phrases like, "Un momentito!" with a huge smile. It warms my heart just thinking about that.

This last example isn't about one specific story, but it's about something amazing she did on a consistent basis. No matter how hard things got, and no matter how much was weighing on her mind, she didn't let anything prevent her from being completely "there" for her family.

I never knew about most of her struggles until I reached adulthood. It was then I found out about some stressful financial investments they'd had, an extensive lawsuit my dad had to handle for his architectural firm, and a series of difficult experiences involving extended family members.

She carried all of those things with such grace.

I'm sure they must have been on her mind while she was baking bread with me or playing our "Polly Wolly Doodle" duet on the piano. Of course she was carrying her own concerns while she washed my cheerleading uniform or drove me to my drama rehearsals, letting me talk all about my homework and tests. But she was so present, so happy, so sweet, and so good at listening that I didn't think for one moment that she had her own burdens to carry. (I wish I could go back and be a greater source of strength to *her*.)

It turns out that every single one of us has feelings of inadequacy and failure. You might even feel like you're failing at something *today*. But when we move forward with persistence, doing what we *can* do, and relying on heaven to lift us, that process brings a level of hope and optimism that few people have the privilege to experience.

If any of us ever feel like we're being pulled down by our inner critic, I hope we'll remember my mom's wise words:

"You must not listen to that negative voice for one minute. If you sit still, you'll hear another voice--a more powerful voice--telling you that you are doing a wonderful job."

> ➤ **QUESTION:** What do you do when your perspective isn't what it needs to be? How do you bring yourself back to center?

> ➤ **CHALLENGE:** Identify one idea that comes to your mind and put it into practice the next time you start to feel that you are failing. I think you'll be amazed by the results!

CHAPTER 24

I Have a Message for You

How complicated is our purpose?

It was deep into the Alzheimer's years, and my sister Laura heard our mom whisper a soft, simple message.

"I *almost* missed it," Laura said. "If I hadn't been listening closely, it would have completely gotten past me. In fact, I didn't realize how profound her message was until I thought about it later that night."

What did she say? Simply this:

"I have a message for you: Love God and love your family."

That's it. So direct. So doable. So central to our deepest purposes in life.

As I think back on these last few years, slowly losing my mother to this disease, that lesson—to love God and love my family—has been reinforced over and over again.

On one Thursday evening visit, while my daughter Alia and I were getting my mom ready for bed, my dad's heart stopped.

Grace and Ethan, who had been with him in the front room, yelled for me to come. Dad was staring straight forward. His body was rigid. There was no breathing. No response. Only a quick gasp or a jerk every couple of seconds, like his body was fighting to live.

143

Alia called the paramedics, I ran to my dad's side to hold him, and through a series of small miracles (including his new pacemaker), he stayed with us.

The part of the experience that impacted me the most, however, happened while I knelt by my dad on the floor of our living room, waiting for the paramedics to arrive.

Not sure if I was ever going to be with him again, I kissed his cheeks and his forehead and said, "I love you, Dad. I love you so much."

He kissed my cheek and replied, "I know you do. And I love you, too."

Such a simple moment, really. But it's one that put everything into perspective for me.

If I were to have lost my dad that night, I would have had zero regrets.

We've been caring for my mom together every Thursday evening *for years.* Together we've gone through all of his photo albums, we've had fun at the beach, we've eaten dinners as a family, and we've laughed at ridiculous memories. He's even listened to me read each of the chapters of this book.

In addition to all of that, we have had a lifetime of beautiful experiences together...vacations as a family, late-night poster-making for my student council campaigns, and hours and hours when I got to snuggle next to him while he read the newspaper or watched TV at night.

We obviously want to make many more memories together, but when the time comes for us to part, I have a powerful feeling of peace—because we're *ready.*

The question now is how we apply that love and devotion to *all* of our most important relationships—especially those with our own children.

Since I started writing this book, my professional life has completely transitioned. My husband and I started a new business together, and while we get to set our own pace and structure our own schedule, I've found that it's hard to step back from my work and just "be" with my family. There's *always* more work to do.

I realized I needed to restructure things, however, when my husband was out of town and our eight-year-old son, Spencer, offered the morning family prayer. He sweetly requested, "Please bless Mommy that she can get her work done today so she can spend time with us."

Of course our children need to understand that we can't play *all* day, but Spencer's sincere request caused me to reflect on this question:

If today were my last day with my husband, one of my children, another member of my extended family, or a dear friend, have I lived my life and prioritized my relationships in such a way that I would feel absolute peace?

My dad always said, "If there is something that needs to change in your life, do it now. Don't wait until tomorrow or the New Year. Make it happen today."

This additional experience my sister Laura shared adds another layer to that perspective:

"One Sunday, during a lesson at church, I was sitting next to Mom, and the discussion centered on qualities we appreciate in a friend. Mom identified the characteristic that she felt was most important: availability. That was so important to her and she lived it—always making herself available to her family and friends."

I don't know if I realized how "available" she made herself while I was growing up, but as I think back, that's all I can remember. I'd rush in the door after school to grab a quick snack and then head back out to another activity. Mom would be sitting at the kitchen table with a smile to welcome me home and a kiss to send me off again. I'd wake up from a Sunday afternoon nap and wander the house looking for her. She'd be waking from her own nap and would open her arms so I could snuggle by her side and talk for a few minutes. I'd call home from my college dorm room, and she would always answer—and talk as long as I wanted.

Because of that example, I've been changing things for the better. I snuggle on the couch with Eric. My phone stays off when I'm talking with my family members. I take Spencer and Ethan rollerblading in the elementary school parking lot as often as I can. I sit in the family room more often, not necessarily *doing* anything, but just being available, I give Grace more back tickles, and I stay up—even when my eyelids are heavy—to hear what's going on with Alia and her friends.

Am I the perfect wife and mother? Or will I *ever* be?

Definitely not.

But the more experiences I have, the more I see that being perfect isn't the point. It's this *trying*—this consistent work in the midst of the "stuff" of life when we get to take care of the people that we love.

The other night, Alia and I sat down at the piano and played *Red River Valley* from the duet book my mom and I loved. Alia has been working on her sight-reading for a few years now, and she played her part *beautifully*.

As memories of duets with my mom flooded into my mind, I said to Alia, "I think I have a video of my mom and I playing this exact same song."

"Go find it!" she exclaimed.

Within moments, I'd serendipitously located the tape, plugged the camera into the television, and started to play the recording from 15 years before.

At that time, Eric and I had a 10-month-old Alia, and we'd just moved to a new city about six hours north of my parents. When the opportunity came for me to take a three-week course to help me run a small home business, I asked my mom if she could come up and take care of Alia for a few days while I attended my classes.

All the worries I felt back then about finances, living in a new city, and transitioning into my role as a mother have faded. There was certainly a lot of anxiety involved, but that was part of my growth.

However, as my family and I watched the video of my young(er), smiling, beautiful mother who knew my name and remembered how to play the piano, I thought, "That moment was one of the greatest treasures of my life."

We have no idea how many years, months, or days we have left with *any* of the precious people we love. I don't want to live my life always feeling stressed about computer work, deadlines, or things that, in the end, don't really matter. I'm guessing you feel the same way.

Our purpose isn't so complicated when we see it with the right perspective. Love God. Love your family. Everything else will fall into place.

➢ *QUESTION:* Thinking about *your* relationships, what would you change if you knew tomorrow were your last day?

➢ *CHALLENGE:* If there is something that needs to change in your life, make that change *now*.

CHAPTER 25

The Beautiful Present

What meaningful moments are right in front of us?

One Thursday evening after dinner, when my mom's memory was *just* starting to go, but she could still walk around the house, my dad said, "I would offer you some ice cream for dessert, but Mother ate all of it."

"I did not!" Mom exclaimed.

"You did, too." Dad teased.

"I can't believe you would say that! That's the meanest thing I think I've ever heard!" she replied with genuine dismay.

I looked across the table at my dad, knowing full well that Mom couldn't remember how many times she'd opened the freezer, and we did our very best to stifle our laughs.

You see, with Alzheimer's, there isn't a past or a future. There's only the present.

Before we, as a family, understood what was going on, we tried to help with the symptoms. Papers, bills, and receipts were strewn across the dining room table, but Mom couldn't grasp the concept of file folders. Her bedroom became an enormous mess, full of straws and napkins she brought home from restaurants—and *dozens* of hand towels she kept buying at the local department store. She apologized over and over again for the lack of order.

I remember spending hours one day organizing her clothing, papers, and personal items into drawers and boxes, only to come back a week later to find the contents of her entire room out in the open again. If she couldn't see it, it didn't exist, and that made her panic.

It worried us privately for years. She couldn't remember when my brother was getting married, so she called our neighbor and pleaded for a ride to the reception—a whole week early. Then she kept losing her cell phone, and it didn't make sense to replace it because we knew she would only lose it again. One afternoon while she was visiting my house, she looked down at her toenails and wondered how on earth they had gotten painted (my girls and I had just finished a little spa treatment for her).

Yes, it's sad to watch someone lose all sense of time, and of course my heart went out to her as I watched her struggle to make sense of her life, but I've come to realize that there is a beautiful gift that comes with Alzheimer's. It's the ability to live fully in the present.

I remember when the forgetfulness was first setting in, and I asked her why she had two perfectly identical Suzy Zoo pocket calendars in her purse.

"Well, this one has all of the birthdays and appointments on it," she said, holding up the first. "And then, if I feel overwhelmed," she said, holding up the second, "I look at this empty one, and I have nothing to do!"

That pretty much left me speechless.

What's been interesting to see, however, is that when all you have is the present, there's no reason not to feel joy.

I called my mom the other day and my dad handed her the phone so she could talk to me from her hospital bed.

"How are you doing, Mom?" I asked.

"Wonderful!" she responded enthusiastically.

"Are you feeling well?"

"Oh yes!"

"Do you know how much I love you?"

"Oh, that's kind of you to say. And I love you too!"

Her life is constant sweetness. She has no idea that she can't walk. No idea that her memory is gone. No worries about politics or financial challenges. It's kind of amazing, when you think about it.

When I visit, I often lower the rail on the side of her bed and climb right in beside her. She puts her arm around me, and I rest my head on her shoulder. In those moments, she isn't worried about her calories or her hair or any upcoming appointments. She doesn't have anywhere to go or anything to do. She is fully mine.

The most difficult part is seeing her, holding her, and kissing her cheeks, but never have the opportunity to open my heart anymore. It often feels like a long, painful, heart-wrenching process of losing my best friend.

However, this is where I need to stop for a moment and consider these questions: if Mom hadn't gotten sick, would I have slowed my pace these past few years and made time with her and with my dad a priority? Would I have developed the same compassion for others who suffer? Would I have written this book about her? Would these memories and experiences have impacted my life as deeply? Would I cherish my husband and children as much as I do now?

To be quite honest, I don't think so.

Whenever we are stretched, something incredible is happening, and one of the best ways we can take advantage of the present is to recognize the meaning that is *literally* right in front of us.

I was extremely sick one Sunday and couldn't get out of bed. My children (especially my then 11-year-old, Grace) took such good care of me. Grace made muffins, cleaned the whole downstairs, and waited on me hand and foot. Seriously, she wouldn't let me do *anything*.

Later that night, while she and I were loading the dishwasher, I said, "Thanks for helping me so much today. You were amazing."

She responded by saying simply this: "If you get old and lose your memory, I want you to know you can trust me."

Alzheimer's requires that you live in the moment—because that's all you really have. How would our lives change if we prioritized the present moments—because that's all that really matters?

Each one of us knows, deep down, that the most important work we will ever do is within our homes and families. We get distracted sometimes, and circumstances can feel hard, but the situations each of us desperately hope will go away are often the ones that bring the most meaning to our lives.

Your children want *you*. Your value is greater than you know. I hope that these stories about my mother can help you to see your life with a clearer perspective because, while her time is drawing to a close, there has never been a better time for us to strengthen the next generation and savor this beautiful present.

> ➤ *QUESTION:* Is there anything in your life that is holding you back from truly living in the present?

> ➤ *CHALLENGE:* Take a moment to consider how a challenge in your life is actually helping you to more fully develop the relationships that are most important.

Conclusion

As I finish writing this book, I picture my mom as she was when I was a teenager—vibrant and healthy, full to the brim with love for her children and everyone around her. Although each time I've told her that I have been writing about her, she responded with surprise and disbelief, I think this book would make her happy because of what she would see in YOU.

I picture her sitting beside you as you read, or as you think about what you've read, stopping to listen if there were any struggles, questions, or thoughts you wanted to share. I can hear her encouraging you to never give up, and I can imagine her wrapping her arms around you—reminding you that you are just the right person for your family—with unique characteristics and abilities.

Maybe your family life wasn't ideal when you were growing up. Or maybe you look at where you are right now, and you wonder what happened to all your beautiful plans. Maybe things are going great, and you're just trying to increase your staying power so you can keep going.

We all have unique challenges, but if there is anything that my mother taught me, it is this: when we devote our very best to the ones who matter most, when we connect with a power that is beyond our own, and when we take care of ourselves so that we thrive (even when it's hard), a sweetness and a hope will come into our lives. I feel that deeply. I know it in my core.

Alzheimer's is slowly bringing my mother's life to an end, but you and I still have the opportunity to make a profound impact within our circles of influence. You have strengths that have uniquely prepared you to fulfill your responsibilities. Your experiences from the past have taught you valuable lessons. You have everything it takes to create an amazing family life and to live your own beautiful Thursdays.

It's exciting to think about, isn't it?

Now, because it breaks my heart to say goodbye, let's not do that.

Instead, please come visit us online and access the wonderful free resources we've prepared to help you strengthen your family. Can't wait to see you there!

http://LearnDoBecome.com/Zoe

Made in the USA
San Bernardino, CA
01 November 2016